W9-BXY-946

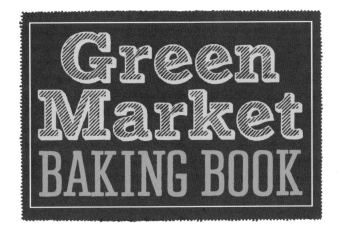

# Green Market
# BAKING BOOK
## 100 Delicious Recipes for Naturally Sweet & Savory Treats

## LAURA C. MARTIN
### with Annie Stilwell Burch and Cameron McCord
### Illustrations by Laura C. Martin

Foreword by PATRICK MARTINS, founder, Slow Food USA

STERLING

New York / London
www.sterlingpublishing.com

Recipes for Coconut Date Rolls (page 168) and Chocolate Tofu (page 170) reprinted from
*The Great American Detox Diet* by Alexandra Jamieson.
Copyright © 2005 by Alexandra Jamieson.
Permission granted by Rodale, Inc., Emmaus, PA 18098.

Mesquite Cornbread recipe (page 144) reprinted from *Native Peoples* magazine.
Permission granted by Beverly Cox.

Fig and Basil Muffins recipe (page 138) reprinted from *Basil: An Herb Lover's Guide* by Thomas Debaggio and
Susan Belsinger, published by Interweave Press, 1996. Permission granted by authors.

Dill Ricotta Torte recipe (page 145) reprinted from *Herbs in the Kitchen* by Carolyn Dille and Susan Belsinger,
published by Interweave Press, 1991. Permission granted by authors.

Vegetable Frittata with Summer Squash, Summer Onion, and Fresh Basil recipe (page 106) reprinted from
*Full Moon Feast* by Jessica Prentice, published in 2006 by Chelsea Green Publishing (www.chelseagreen.com).
Permission granted by author.

STERLING and the distinctive Sterling logo are registered trademarks of
Sterling Publishing Co., Inc.

**Library of Congress Cataloging-in-Publication Data Available**

10  9  8  7  6  5  4  3  2  1

Published by Sterling Publishing Co., Inc.
387 Park Avenue South, New York, NY 10016
© 2011 by Laura C. Martin
Distributed in Canada by Sterling Publishing
*C/o* Canadian Manda Group, 165 Dufferin Street
Toronto, Ontario, Canada M6K 3H6
Distributed in the United Kingdom by GMC Distribution Services
Castle Place, 166 High Street, Lewes, East Sussex, England BN7 1XU
Distributed in Australia by Capricorn Link (Australia) Pty. Ltd.
P.O. Box 704, Windsor, NSW 2756, Australia

*Printed in China*
*All rights reserved*

Sterling ISBN 978-1-4027-5997-0

For information about custom editions, special sales, premium and
corporate purchases, please contact Sterling Special Sales
Department at 800-805-5489 or specialsales@sterlingpublishing.com.

To our family,

especially Jack, Michael, and Andy

# Contents

# Foreword

EVER SINCE THE EIGHTEENTH CENTURY, TO BE SLOW WAS TO OBSTRUCT progress and civilization. Nature's secrets were unlocked and we discovered her quicksilver side: electricity, the speed of light, the incomprehensible whirl of subatomic particles. We built our modern society upon the assumption that speed is equivalent to efficiency and that efficiency is equivalent to "saving" time, as if seconds can be hoarded and spent later. Progress was good. Faster was better.

Thanks in part to the Slow Food movement, our culture has reevaluated the implications of "slow." Now "taking" time can be as worthwhile as "saving" it, whether seeking out a small business that specializes in a craft or baking a pie with family and friends using fruits from the local farmers' market. Without challenging its value, we now recognize a more sophisticated understanding of efficiency. It is an understanding that, perhaps unsurprisingly, restores our respect for natural rhythms.

The fast-faster-fastest emphasis of commodity culture, coupled with the relentlessness of globalization, fills our world with both frenzy and glut. Many companies have moved faster than their ability to produce decent products. Witness 2007, the "Year of the Recall." Factory farming, mad cow disease, and E. coli spread when reckless speed and profit-seeking trumped sounder, but slower, values. When consumers are dying and the environment is being ravished, when workers' rights are compromised and community bonds are dissolving—all as a consequence of our fast-faster-fastest method of doing business—the results can hardly be construed as efficient for our society as a whole.

The traditions and simplicity of growing and eating food in time-tested ways have become a mere memory. The fast-faster-fastest mentality is marked by ignoring the qualities people cherish most in order to promote those aspects of a commodity that make it more valuable to store, ship, and sell. Simply proposing an alternative to the global economy will not work—"global alternatives" are abstract figments. The only true alternatives are those that exist within the domain of personal choice. Business practice conforms to the international economy that has emerged like a constellation from the accumulation of millions of personal choices made across the planet every day. The only way we can create change is to work within that economy, and the only way we will succeed in influencing personal choices is by influencing the value system people draw upon when making those choices.

Laura Martin's book describes in great and delicious detail a choice that is very different from those proposed by the world's richest food companies. The proliferation of artificial sweeteners, processed chemicals, and high levels of refined sugars in store-bought food is a tragic circumstance sanctioned by those in power, one that has turned this generation into the first ever to not live longer than the one that preceded it. The answer to satisfying your sweet tooth without poisoning your body is to use local and seasonal fruits, vegetables, and herbs, along with whole grains and natural sweeteners. By eating like this, your destiny is in your hands, and the result is a healthier body, a healthier environment, and healthier local food communities.

Sweets are the very definition of pleasure, and taking the time to bake with family and friends is a way of prolonging that pleasure. I assure you that you will love reading and making the recipes in this book, from Chef Linton Hopkins's honey whole wheat or rosemary olive breads, to Alice Waters's famous whole wheat waffles.

The fast-faster-fastest business of commodities makes similar, but lesser, versions of products and charges little for them, burying the true cost of their charade in a tab that they expect society—and the environment—to pay. By reading this book you will support a virtuous production system, include a little sweetness in your life, and find great recipes that you won't have to pay for later.

—*Patrick Martins, founder, Slow Food USA*

# Introduction

THE IDEA FOR THIS BOOK BEGAN WITH THE MOST ANCIENT OF ALL experiences—a family sharing a meal together. The "slow food" bug bit our large, complicated family and we're enthusiastic about eating things that are locally grown. An excursion to the local farmers' market became one of the highlights of our week.

The meals we fixed from the treasures we found were fabulous, but there was always something missing. After a feast of green beans, fresh corn on the cob, heirloom tomatoes, yellow squash, fried okra, and eggplant, we congratulated ourselves on being "locavores" and eating a meal completely locally grown. Then someone asked about dessert. Silence. Blueberry pie, someone suggested. No, sugar isn't local! Raspberry sorbet? Same answer. Peach cobbler? Oatmeal cookies? Blackberry tart? Same answer. Isn't there anything a little more decadent than just locally grown fruit that we can have for dessert?

Since we didn't have the answer, we turned to our friends in the food world for help. We posed this question: "Can you bake with local ingredients from small producers and create things that taste good without using sugar?"

The answer was an emphatic "Yes!" and the recipes began pouring in. The bakers who responded used natural sweeteners, fresh fruits and vegetables, and nuts and grains in innovative and delicious ways to make everything from cookies to cakes, pies to pastries. Some bakers used locally produced honey or maple syrup, but others went farther afield and used ingredients such as agave nectar and brown rice syrup. While these are not local, they are natural and helped us avoid using corn syrup and refined sugar, thus supporting small family producers instead of the giant sugar industry.

These recipes were so absolutely delicious that we became a little greedy and asked other chefs and bakers to contribute; the response was tremendous. We quickly realized that these recipes were just too good to keep to ourselves. The result is the *Green Market Baking Book,* a collection of recipes from people excited about creating the best food possible in the most conscientious way they can. To borrow the motto of Slow Food, an international organization founded in 1986 to counteract fast food and fast life, these are people who bake food that is "good, clean, and fair."

Our contributors shared their recipes with grace and uncommon generosity. Some, such as Alice Waters, Tom Douglas, and Dan Barber, are known internationally. Others enjoy more local fame, but each has a passion for good food made with fresh, seasonal ingredients, baked in a way that is good for our bodies, good for our communities, and good for our Earth.

This book could not be timelier. During the past few years, we have seen an astounding increase in interest in eating locally, seasonally, and healthfully. According to the USDA, the number of farmers' markets in the country increased by 13 percent between 2008 and 2009, with over five thousand currently in operation. Membership in organizations such as Slow Food has swelled. To date, there are more than 100,000 members of Slow Food International in 132 countries.

While there are many cookbooks dedicated to the idea of eating locally, most of these offer recipes for cooking with fresh ingredients such as carrots and turnips. Without speaking poorly of carrots and turnips, we feel that it's easier to encourage people to eat healthfully and locally with a hot apple pie rather than turnip stew, or with carrot *cake* rather than carrot *juice*. We think that yummy baked things should be a part of every celebration—and that people should celebrate often.

The whole family was involved in this book. My daughter-in-law, Annie Burch Stilwell and my daughter, Cameron McCord, were particularly helpful in choosing and testing the recipes, and everyone else "worked" hard tasting different recipes, doing their job with great enthusiasm.

We offer you this collection of recipes from the best chefs and bakers in the business. Each recipe has been tested and tasted and retested and exclaimed over and devoured with gusto. It is our hope that you will find that these are some of the most delicious things you've ever baked. We won't claim that this will be the answer to global warming—but it might get us a step closer to world peace. After all, how can you argue while eating the world's best hot apple pie?

—*Laura Martin (the Green Market Baker)*

*All recipes not marked with a contributor are from the Green Market Baker.*

# Answers to a Few Questions

THIS BOOK WAS BORN FROM A DESIRE TO GIVE PEOPLE ALTERNATIVES to baking with refined sugar and artificial sugar products, and to encourage them to support their local food communities. Because sugar (under various guises, including cane sugar, high fructose corn syrup [or hfcs], sucrose, fructose, etc.) is in so many of our prepared foods (including ketchup, mayonnaise, salad dressing, crackers, bread, and the million other things that you would *expect* to contain sugar), almost all of us are eating too much sugar.

Eliminating sweets from our diets is not our favorite solution to this problem. Instead, we have found ways to bake with healthful ingredients, to . . . well, have our cake and eat it, too. Although we're quite aware that eating too much of any kind of sweetener is not good for us, we are excited to have found a way to continue to bake and eat decadently, support our local food community, and maintain our health.

. . . . . . .

## Definitions

In this "new" green world, it's sometimes hard to keep up with the latest catchword. Eavesdrop on a conversation at your local market or at a gathering of Slow Food and you'll hear terms such as *organic, sustainable, green,* and *natural* tossed about. For many people, these terms are confusing.

ORGANIC For a long time, the word *organic* was used to refer to food that was grown without pesticides, but eventually it came to mean—or at least indicate—much more. For example, in the past, it was difficult for large-scale farmers to grow organically, so, by association, *organic* implied small farm or small producer as well.

Since many small farms are run by families or friends who have banded together to work the land, most of us assumed that they treat each other and their workers well and that *organic*, again by association, meant *fair trade*.

And, of course, the best way for small farmers to sell their produce was to sell it to their neighbors or nearby restaurants, so *organic* even indicated *local*.

But even though there are a lot of vague associations with the term, the designation *organic* is actually quite precise. To sell "organic" products in the United States, the producer must be certified through the National Organic Program. Certification is based on farming in a way that maintains and replenishes soil fertility without the use of toxic and persistent pesticides and fertilizers. Becoming certified is a long and expensive process, and many farmers choose not to pursue certification, but to follow similar farming practices, working to treat the land with respect so that it is not harmed in any way.

When I asked Chef Linton Hopkins in Atlanta if he bought from only organic farmers, he shook his head no and answered, "The philosophy and ethics of the farmer are more important to me than the certification." And then he added that he personally knew most of his farmers.

The way Linton knows his farmers is the same way that more and more top chefs (and home cooks) know the people who produce their food—they buy locally.

LOCAL Perhaps of all those terms, *local* is both the most readily understood and least definable. *Local* to some people means within a certain number of miles. For example, the San Francisco "Eat Local Challenge" encourages people to eat food produced within 250 miles of San Francisco. But here in Georgia, we're faced with a different set of circumstances. Alice Rolls, executive director of Georgia Organics, says "I don't really like to put a mileage limit on 'local' because we don't have the luxury in terms of supply, particularly here in the South. Some people use 'a day's drive' to define it, which is handily nebulous!"

It is probably sufficient to say that *local* means food that is grown as close to home as possible. Tomatoes from a backyard garden are extremely local no matter where you live. For Georgians, strawberries from Florida are probably more "regional" than local, but still better than buying strawberries from California. For most of us, *local* means buying close to home to reduce environmental impact and to support the local farming community.

SUSTAINABLE *Sustainable*, too, is easily defined, though the implications are far-reaching. A working definition of sustainable agriculture is "a way of growing crops that addresses both the profitability of farms and preserving the environment." *Sustainable* today also means the fair treatment of workers and the humane treatment of animals.

GREEN *Green* is no longer just a color. *Green* today means a mind-set and a way of life. To live *green* means to live your life with consideration and sensitivity to your personal impact on the environment. Food choices play a tremendous part in one's ability to interact with the environment in a positive way—or at least to do as little harm as possible.

NATURAL Eating *natural*, in terms of food, means avoiding foods that are made in a laboratory (margarine is an example of such a non-food) and, instead, enjoying the abundance of the earth and the foods that are naturally produced from it. An easy gauge is this: If people living a century ago wouldn't recognize something as food, then it's probably not real food.

Even if you understand the definitions of these terms, you still may not "get" why buying local, natural, seasonal, and organic food is so important. After all, in most cases, food like this not only costs a lot more, it doesn't last as long as packaged food. So what's the big deal?

## Why Local?

There are many reasons to buy foods that are produced close to where you live, although there is some controversy about the environmental benefits of doing so. Based purely on mathematics, mega-farms produce food more efficiently than smaller farms and it is possible to argue that this efficiency more than makes up for the cost of the fuel used in transportation. But economics and math aside, there are other, not-so-controversial reasons for buying local products, including supporting small farmers instead of big business, as well as issues of taste and freshness.

Almost all produce tastes best when freshly picked. Anyone who has eaten a freshly picked tomato would agree with that. If you can get produce that was picked hours or even days before, it is going to taste better than things that have been

sitting in a refrigerated truck for a week or more. This is definitely true for produce that is eaten raw, but is also true for baking and cooking. The fresher the produce, the better the final outcome.

Farmers who grow produce for a fresh market (such as a farmers' market) instead of a mass market (such as a grocery store) can grow vegetables and fruit bred for taste rather than for the ability to withstand long shipping times. Heritage or heirloom varieties grown for home consumption or for a small market have more delicious and distinctive flavors than the varieties found at large chain supermarkets.

When you buy local food from nearby small farms, it is comforting to know where your food is grown and how it is processed. Not only will you have a better feeling about what you're eating and feeding your family, you'll also have the satisfaction of knowing that you are contributing to your local food community and that you are taking part in the kind of food chain that humans have participated in for millennia. You may not be able to trade milk for eggs, like my grandmother did, but by buying locally and supporting the neighborhood food community, you become a vital element in its stability.

## Why Seasonal?

Only during the last century have we been able to eat fresh food *out* of season. Although it's nice to have lettuce in February and strawberries in September, these should be treats rather than staples. Our bodies need different kinds of foods during different times of the year. In spring, when we need rejuvenating after a long winter, the fresh, new growth of leafy vegetables is just what the doctor ordered. It's no coincidence that this is the season of lettuce, arugula, collards, chard, and many other leafy vegetables.

In contrast, during winter, our bodies need more filling, warming foods—in general, vegetables that take longer to grow. Again, it's no coincidence that the late fall harvest includes slow growers such as potatoes, carrots, onions, and nuts.

There are economic and practical reasons for eating in season as well. Produce that has just been recently harvested is fresher, probably locally grown, more abundant, and usually less expensive.

## Why Organic?

Perhaps the question should be: Why would you choose *non*-organic goods? Why would you choose produce, meats, eggs, and poultry that have been pumped full of harmful materials and sprayed with chemicals known to be poisonous? There are reasons, of course, the most important being cost, availability, and convenience—

but, oh, what a price we pay in terms of our own health, the environmental degradation, and the health and well-being of farm workers.

No doubt about it, items that are conventionally grown are less expensive, at least in the short term. But in terms of long-term health care for ourselves and our children, buying organic is a superb investment. The number of toxins present in our foods is sickening—literally. Children are particularly vulnerable to these toxins. Kids today experience much greater exposure to many widely used, cancer-causing pesticides than children did a generation ago.

Fortunately, organic products are becoming more widely available and less expensive. Some people believe that large-scale "organic" farming operations threaten the livelihoods of small farmers who have depended on "organic" to give them a competitive edge. That may be true, but the survival of the "little guy" is a different issue from that of the increase of organic goods available to us. From a health viewpoint, the more organic, the better.

Farming organically helps air and water quality, lessens soil erosion, and protects farm workers by eliminating exposure to harmful chemicals. It also helps reduce dependence on oil. Modern farms use more fuel than any other industry in the United States and, of this amount, nearly a third is used in the manufacture of chemical fertilizers.

Buying organic products is not just a fad and not just the concern of liberals or "tree huggers." More and more, organic is becoming mainstream—and staying there. It is good for our bodies and our environment.

## Why No Sugar?

The chefs who contributed recipes to the *Green Market Baking Book* use local, seasonal produce and natural sweeteners. This is how we all should bake and it is how our mothers *should* have baked. It's the same way their mother should have baked, and so on. Actually, if you go back far enough, you'll find mothers that actually did bake this way. You'd have to go back several centuries, though, because by the eighteenth century Europeans were eating a large quantity of refined sugar, and processed foods were soon to follow.

But never in history have people consumed so much sugar in so many different and potentially detrimental forms as they do today. Refined sugar is made from a natural plant, either sugar cane or sugar beets, but is so highly processed that by the time it gets into the sugar bowl, you can't tell which plant it came from. In addition, the refining process uses chemicals you don't want in your body, including calcium hydroxide (lime) and carbon dioxide. To top it off, sugar is bleached using charred animal bones.

Of course, we Green Market Bakers avoid corn syrup as well as refined sugar. Corn syrup, or high fructose corn syrup (sometimes referred to as hfcs), is even more prevalent in processed foods than sugar is because it is so cheap.

Refined sugar is primarily sucrose; corn syrup is primarily fructose. There is abundant information about the differences between the two, but in the end both are empty calories that end up triggering a spike in blood sugar and that contribute greatly to diabetes and obesity.

So if you're not diabetic and you're not overweight, what's wrong with using refined sugar? There are countless claims that sugar is detrimental to the body, contributing to everything from diabetes to weak eyesight, eczema to yeast infections, but, of course, there are also countless claims (particularly from the sugar industry) saying that sugar is a "natural" food and that it's okay to have up to 25 percent of your daily caloric intake be from sugar.

And here is where we jump feet-first into the politics of food, with activists and health experts on one side and big business on the other side. Sound familiar? Remember the tobacco industry claiming for years that smoking was not detrimental to your health?

Of course there are extremists on both sides, but since it has been proven that sugar is a culprit in the onset of some of the most deadly diseases that are attacking our children—juvenile diabetes and obesity—it should be avoided at all costs. Literally.

Refined sugar is cheap, which is why it is used in so many processed foods. It is also addictive, meaning the more you eat, the more you want, which, again, is why it is ubiquitous in processed foods. Natural sweeteners are not cheap, but they are also not as addictive as processed sugar and corn syrup, and most do contain trace amounts of nutrients.

One of the biggest reasons we, personally, have eliminated refined sugar from our diets, though, is that it makes us think twice about eating most processed foods. Since so many of them contain sugar, we just don't eat them. The result is that we make many more things from scratch, and frankly, it takes both time and effort to make these things, so we don't eat them in the same quantities. It's been a very effective means of cutting back.

But we're definitely not interested in cutting out sweets altogether. According to Traditional Chinese Medicine (and common sense), we all need sweetness in our lives. We need six tastes—sweet, sour, salty, astringent, bitter, and pungent—to stimulate the taste buds on our tongue at meals in order to be satisfied. If we're not satisfied, we're going to crave the things that are missing. So it's really not possible to just give up on sweets. Instead, we suggest that you try a whole new way of eating desserts, using locally produced, sustainable whole foods such as natural sweeteners, whole grains, and delicious, fresh seasonal produce.

We realize that the natural sweeteners we use in our recipes (maple syrup, honey, brown rice syrup, barley malt syrup, and agave nectar) should still be used in moderation. They are ingredients that are full of calories and contain few nutrients. Honey and maple syrup, like processed sugar, spike blood sugar levels. We do feel that the natural sweeteners are healthier alternatives, but we advocate their use in moderation.

## Why Natural?

The idea of an "unnatural" food would have been a little bizarre to our ancestors. Eating something that was made of lab chemicals and that was artificially made to look like real food would have earned the reaction it should—incredulity and a little disgust.

One of the first "fake foods" was margarine, which was developed by the French chemist Hippolyte Mège-Mouriès, who made a substitute for butter out of beef suet and milk. Over the years, these original ingredients have been replaced with other things. Marion Nestle, in her excellent book *What to Eat* (2006), says that "No matter what their labels say, all margarines are basically the same—mixtures of soybean oil and food additives. Everything else is theater and greasepaint."

You might think that there is nothing wrong with soybean oil and you might be right, though that's a whole other issue (check out Butter and Oils on pages 20–23). But, the oil used in margarine today needs to be hydrogenated to make it a solid (soybean oil is a liquid at room temperature) and the hydrogenation process creates unhealthful trans fats, making it a much different product from just plain soy oil.

There are many advantages to eating whole foods. One is that they taste delicious; another is that you'll know precisely what you are putting into your body. Imagine a food chart that shows how far from the original plant or animal a particular food is. Spinach is a basic, primary food. An egg is only once removed. Margarine, on the other hand, is far from the source (soybeans). The original plant product is mixed with a wide variety of chemicals, pumped full of hydrogen (which changes its essential chemical structure), dyed and whipped, and finally put into a plastic tub for our consumption. Margarine in no way resembles the original food source. The closer to the earth we eat, the healthier we will be.

Eating naturally is also a way to support small producers—the vegetable farmers and millers, the dairy farmers and beekeepers—because these are people who produce the real foods our bodies need.

# The Ingredients

ONE INSPIRATION FOR WRITING THIS BOOK IS THE FABULOUS LOCAL AND seasonal ingredients that are becoming increasingly available to all of us. To make the most delicious baked goods possible, you need good recipes to begin with, of course, but the better the ingredients, the better the results. The best ingredients are those that are fresh, organic, and high quality. We also believe that the best ingredients are made with sensitivity to nature, to the people who work to produce the goods, and to the animals.

This section includes information about ingredients used in the recipes, including organic produce, natural sweeteners, grains and flours, fats and oils (butter and various vegetable and nut oils), and dairy products.

· · · · · · ·

## Produce

Fresh produce is the heart of the green market and the glory of these recipes, but when buying produce you are faced with many decisions. Do you buy organic? Local? Fair trade? Or, if you can't do all of the above, which are most important?

There are no rigid rules governing these choices. Much of it depends on circumstances, individual preference, and your knowledge of the farmers who produce your food. I usually buy from a local farmer, even though he isn't certified organic. I know he doesn't use chemicals on his gardens, but he can't get certified because the fence around the property is made from treated wood. To me, that is a risk worth taking.

Sometimes, the limiting factor for buying organic is money—there's no question about it, organic produce is usually more expensive. If you can't afford to buy all your groceries from an organic, local farmer, how do you prioritize? Which foods are the most important to buy organic? Or, looking at it from the opposite side, which fruits and vegetables retain the greatest amounts of toxins from pesticides and should *only* be eaten when they're grown organically?

The Environmental Working Group, a nonprofit environmental research organization dedicated to improving public health and protecting the environment, has ranked common fruits and vegetables based on their tendency to retain toxins.

Their advice? "The best option is to eat a varied diet, wash all produce, and choose organic when possible to reduce exposure to potentially harmful chemicals. Peeling also reduces exposures, but valuable nutrients often go down the drain with the peel." (From the Environmental Working Group website, www.ewg.org.)

The following is a list of the Environmental Working Group's "dirty dozen," with the worst offenders listed first, meaning you should try to choose organic over conventionally farmed varieties:

Peaches

Apples

Bell peppers

Celery

Nectarines

Strawberries

Cherries

Kale

Lettuce

Grapes (imported)

Carrots

Pears

For more information about produce, check out the seasonal chapters, which include information about seasonal produce and how to choose, prepare, store, and, of course, bake with the best of the season.

## Natural Sweeteners

We love sweets. I mean, we LOVE sweets, but we know that sugar is extremely detrimental to our health. We also know that refined sugar is almost always produced by large international corporations and we're all about supporting small farms. So we don't use refined sugar, preferring to use a wide variety of sweeteners created by small producers and, when possible, using locally produced goods.

What can you use instead of white sugar? Lots—there are many natural alternatives to choose from. For those pledged to eating as locally as possible, honey is the best sugar alternative because there are beekeepers in almost every community. You can also use maple syrup, maple sugar, agave nectar, brown rice syrup, date sugar, and barley malt syrup (or, better yet, a combination of these) in place of sugar.

Although many people use stevia (a sweetener that comes from the leaves of the stevia plant, which you can actually grow in your garden), we think it's hard to bake with. We also feel that, even though it is "natural," it is still a highly processed food. Granted, it is low in calories, which the above-mentioned sweeteners are not. Erythritol, a sugar alcohol found in many fruits and some mushrooms, is also low in calories but is a highly processed product and difficult to use in baking. Xylitol, a sweetener made from the birch tree, is tricky and best used in small amounts in hot beverages rather than in baking.

Chemical sweeteners, of which there are seemingly countless numbers, are not a viable choice for those of us who advocate eating whole, natural foods and who are conscientious about our health.

HONEY Although most honey looks about the same, differing only in shades of amber brown that range from dark to light, there are a wide variety of honey tastes and flavors, depending on the source of nectar. In general, light-colored honey has a more delicate flavor and is better for baking than dark-colored honey, which can be quite robust and heavily flavored.

---

### Types of Honey

**Mild-flavored honey**
alfalfa, clover, orange, wildflower

**More flavorful honey**
tupelo, blackberry, sourwood, mesquite

---

Bees produce honey from nectar gathered from a dominant, though not exclusive, flower source. There are more than three hundred different types of honeys in the United States, clover being the most common. In our home state of Georgia, we are blessed with an abundance of flowering plants, and bees produce many different delicious kinds of honey, including blackberry, gallberry, orange blossom, sourwood, sumac, tulip poplar, cotton, tupelo, and even the scourge of the South, kudzu.

Wildflower honey (which is often less expensive than single-flower honeys) is produced from nectar from a variety of flowers when there is no clear, dominant source. Wildflower honey changes as the seasons progress. Spring wildflower honey tastes distinctly different from fall wildflower honey because different flowers are in bloom.

"Raw" or unfiltered, unrefined, and unprocessed honey is considered the highest quality and is best appreciated when eaten as a condiment. When baking with honey, buying "raw" is not as critical since it will be heated anyway. According to Ayurvedic medicine, the beneficial properties of honey are destroyed when it is heated (as in baking) and it actually contributes to mucus formation. If this is important to you, choose a different sweetener when baking.

Be aware that cheap honey is sometimes mixed with other ingredients, so be sure you are purchasing pure honey.

Honey has 65 calories per tablespoon. It is a simple sugar that is quickly absorbed by the body and thus is not good for those with blood sugar issues. Honey does contain trace amounts of minerals and enzymes, though usually not enough to be considered significant.

When measuring honey, oil the measuring cup before pouring in the honey. This allows the honey to slide out smoothly and quickly, making for more accurate measurements and much faster cleanup.

Store honey at room temperature, not in the refrigerator. Refrigeration causes it to crystallize faster.

**Note:** *Do not give raw honey to children under the age of one (some pediatricians say two). Honey may contain the spores of the bacteria that cause botulism, which can germinate in immature digestive systems. These spores are not harmful to older children and adults.*

**AGAVE NECTAR** This is a liquid sweetener that comes from the blue agave plants in Mexico (the same genus of plants that give us tequila). It's a desert succulent, similar to a cactus.

Studies conducted in 2009 indicate that agave is not as healthy an alternative sweetener as once hoped. The process by which the starchy tuber is converted to a liquid is similar to the chemical process that changes corn starch to HFCS. The result is a syrup that is 90 precent fructose.

Dark agave syrup tastes a little like maple syrup, but the light version offers sweetness with very little flavoring and is great in hot beverages such as tea or coffee or for sweetening unflavored soy milk. Because it is so lightly flavored it's good for making sauces and custards when you want other flavors to shine.

**BROWN RICE SYRUP** Brown rice syrup has a butterscotch-like flavor. At 75 calories per tablespoon, it is one of the more caloric natural sweeteners, especially when you consider that it is much less sweet than sugar, so you need more to get the same sweetness. Even so, it is considered one of the most healthful of all the sweeteners. The traditional method for making this syrup is to combine sprouted barley with brown rice and cook it until the starch has turned into sugar. Made this way, the syrup is absorbed by the body very slowly, making it good to use in recipes for people with blood sugar issues. Brown rice syrup made this way will be labeled "sprouted barley," "sprouted rice," or "malted rice."

Some manufacturers isolate enzymes from sprouted barley instead of using the whole barley. This results in a syrup that is much higher in glucose, which is absorbed by the body more quickly. These labels say "brown rice, barley, water" or sometimes "cereal enzymes." The difference between the two methods is substantial. Whenever you can, use brown rice syrup processed the traditional way.

Store brown rice syrup in a cool, dry place.

If you are gluten-intolerant, be sure to look for brown rice syrup that is marked "gluten-free."

**BARLEY MALT SYRUP** This syrup has a malty, molasses flavor and is made from sprouted barley, mixed with water and cooked grains. It contains about 60 calories per tablespoon and is high in maltose and low in glucose. It is good in foods that can handle its robust flavor, such as muffins, cakes, and sweet breads. Barley malt syrup does contain gluten and should be avoided by those who are sensitive to gluten or suffer from celiac disease.

MAPLE SYRUP One of the most used natural sweeteners, maple syrup has been utilized in traditional cooking for hundreds of years. When European settlers first came to America, they learned the trick of tapping the sweet sap of the maple tree from Native Americans.

At 52 calories per tablespoon, it is less caloric than many of the other sweeteners, but because it has a relatively high sucrose content the body absorbs it in the same manner as sugar. It is not recommended for people with blood sugar issues and should be used by everyone in moderation. The advantages to using it over refined sugar are: (1) taste, (2) it can be purchased from a small producer or "farmer," (3) it does contain trace amounts of nutrients, (4) it is minimally processed, and (5) even though it has a high sucrose content, it's still only two-thirds the sucrose of sugar.

Maple syrup is great for blending with other sweeteners. Because maple syrup produces a crisp product and other sweeteners (honey, agave nectar, barley malt, and brown rice syrups) produce moist goods, combining maple syrup with other natural sweeteners provides a balance.

Maple syrup is graded according to color and flavor. Grade A comes in light, medium, and dark and is considered a superior product. Grade B is even darker. Not being a real maple syrup connoisseur (I'm from Georgia!), I prefer the delicious, robust Grade B, which has the added advantage of being slightly cheaper.

Once opened, maple syrup should be stored in the refrigerator, particularly if you live in a hot climate. Although it often comes in tins or plastic containers, ideally maple syrup should be stored in glass to avoid contamination. It will last for many months.

MAPLE SUGAR Granulated maple syrup can be substituted equally for refined white sugar. It is extremely good yet extremely expensive, but for certain things it's worth the price. One of my favorite recipes in this book is the Green Market Baking Book Chocolate Chip Cookies recipe (see page 31). Using maple sugar was the only way we could find to get the crisp *and* the chew in this cookie.

Store granulated maple sugar in a cool, dry place. It will keep for up to twelve months.

DATE SUGAR This is made from ground dehydrated dates and can be used like brown sugar in many recipes. Because it does not dissolve in hot liquids, it is not used as a sweetener in coffee or tea. Date sugar is particularly useful when you want to *see* something that looks like sugar—like a streusel topping or a fruit crisp, or on top of cereal.

SORGHUM Sorghum syrup is a natural sweetener made from the grain *Sorghum bicolor* (which is also the source of an excellent flour—see the following section on grains). Sorghum syrup tastes a lot like molasses (which is a by-product of sugar manufacturing and which we have declined to use in this book). Since it takes about eight gallons of sorghum juice to make one gallon of syrup, sorghum syrup is expensive, but it's a great local sweetener for those who live in the South where sorghum is grown commercially.

Each different sweetener has its benefits: Maple syrup has the fewest calories. Honey, brown rice, and barley malt syrup all contain trace amounts of nutrients. Honey is the most available locally. Agave nectar is sweet without a heavy flavor, is not too expensive, and contains a (relatively) moderate number of calories. It mixes well with honey and maple syrup. Combining any of these increases the complexity of the sugars and usually enhances the taste. For information about substituting these sweeteners in various recipes, see pages 26–34.

## Grains and Flours

Almost anything you bake is going to use some sort of grain; it's as simple as that. You may use flour that is gluten-free or full of gluten, flour that is yellow, white, brown, or blue, or flour that is made from any number of different grains, including both modern and ancient. The variety of flours available is staggering. But the bottom line is that baked goods, from pies to pastries, cookies to cupcakes, biscotti to bread, almost always include some kind of flour or grain.

Talk about "whole grains" is ubiquitous. The phrase is plastered on everything from cereal boxes to bags of pasta. Whole grain means just that—it is a product that includes everything present in the seed or grain of a cereal plant. The seed is made of three parts:

**1.** Bran—the outside covering of the seed; rich in fiber and B vitamins (such as wheat bran or rice bran)

**2.** Germ—the part of the seed that actually sprouts to make a new plant; rich in vitamin E and B vitamins (such as wheat germ)

**3.** Endosperm—largest part of the seed; full of carbohydrates and proteins

If you eat a whole grain, you get all the goodies from each part of the seed. However, you still need to be a savvy consumer. Many products that now claim to be "whole grain" also claim to be good for you, but make sure you look at the other ingredients when purchasing products that have labels shouting "whole grain!" Many of these products are full of fats and sugars. Even better than checking a label, though, just bake it yourself.

Whole grains are indisputably better for you than refined grains. Margaret M. Wittenberg, in her book *New Good Food* (2007), says "Eating whole grains can also reduce the risk of diabetes, obesity, and stroke; epidemiological studies even indicate that it reduces early mortality rates." Make mine whole grain!

**Storing Flours**
Flour generally has a pretty short shelf life unless it is stored correctly. This is particularly true of the many non-gluten flours such as rice or sorghum flour. It's best to store all whole grains in airtight containers in a cool place (less than 70 degrees). The easiest way to do this is to store the flours in the refrigerator or the freezer if you have room.

**Flours that Contain Gluten**
To most people, flour is synonymous with wheat and therefore with gluten, and for good reason. Wheat has been used for millennia to make the most delicious baked goods imaginable—from flaky piecrusts to rich aromatic breads, from delicate, crumbly cakes to crisp cookies. These are made possible by the gluten protein complex found within the wheat.

There are many different kinds of wheat flours available to us. They vary depending on when and where the crop was grown, the color of the wheat, and how it was harvested and processed. The bran, or the outside of the kernel, gives the wheat its color—and the wheat kernel can be white, amber, or red. In the United States, red wheat is the most common, though white wheat is making inroads because it offers bakers a white-colored whole-grain flour that is a little sweeter than the traditional brown whole wheat. In addition to color, wheat flour can also be marked as hard or soft, winter or spring, whole grain, bleached or unbleached, pastry, cake, bread, self-rising, or all-purpose, among other classifications.

All these different wheat flours have advantages and disadvantages, but for our purposes—that of baking with the most healthful ingredients possible—we recommend that you don't buy self-rising or bleached flour. We found that it was possible to substitute whole wheat pastry flour for all-purpose flour in most recipes for cookies, cakes, and pastries.

DURUM FLOUR Durum flour is a hard wheat with a high percentage of protein; it is yellowish in color. Semolina is a type of durum flour that is most often used for making pasta. Durum flour is most often used in combination with other flours to add texture and taste to breads.

**WHOLE WHEAT FLOUR** Whole wheat flour is a robust, full-grain flour in which the whole kernel, including the bran, endosperm, and germ, is ground to produce the flour. Baking with whole wheat flour alone results in dense, heavy breads or other baked goods. To lighten things up a bit you can either use whole wheat pastry flour or combine whole wheat flour with unbleached all-purpose flour. Whole wheat flour tends to absorb more liquid than white flour. Since too much liquid is almost always a problem when maple syrup, honey, or other moist sweeteners are substituted for dry white sugar, this "problem" is actually an advantage for natural bakers.

Whole wheat pastry flour is made from the whole kernel of soft wheat, but has less gluten than regular whole wheat flour. It's great for pastries (thus the name), cookies, muffins, and piecrusts.

White whole wheat flour is a pale yellow flour that offers the advantage of that "lily white" look that is difficult to obtain with brown whole wheat flour. It is high in gluten and is good for making breads, cookies, quick breads, cakes, etc. (In spite of its light color, I'm not a big fan of white whole wheat. It often has a gritty texture to it that I find unappealing.)

**UNBLEACHED ALL-PURPOSE FLOUR** Unbleached all-purpose flour is not as healthful as a whole-grain flour, but our recipe contributors use a lot of it. Where possible, we've suggested substituting at least part of the amount of white flour with a whole-grain alternative. All-purpose flour makes a light, fluffy batter or dough. For more information about substituting different flours, see pages 34–35.

**RYE FLOUR** Rye is closely related to barley and wheat and does contain gluten. It is usually ground into flour and used in breads, particularly dark breads such as pumpernickel. Rye is common in Eastern European cuisine because of the large quantity grown there.

**SPELT FLOUR** Spelt is another wheat relative that contains gluten, though many people with a gluten intolerance can eat spelt more easily than wheat. Spelt also tends to absorb more moisture in cooking than wheat, making it a good addition in recipes using liquid natural sweeteners. It is high in protein and is easily digested.

### Gluten-Free Flours

**AMARANTH** Considered the sacred food of the Aztecs, amaranth has been around for about five thousand years. Technically, it is not a grain, as it does not belong to the cereal family. Amaranth has enjoyed a recent revival in popularity due to its nutritional value. Because it contains lysine, a type of amino acid, it provides a high-quality, complete protein. In addition, it is rich in calcium. It is particularly good to mix with other flours as it is gluten-free.

It has a slightly nutty, spicy flavor and produces a moist crumb and a crisp crust. If you include amaranth in baked goods, you might have to bake things a little longer than normal. You can grow your own amaranth but beware, it is hardy and can become invasive.

Use in pancakes, muffins, and cookies.

**BUCKWHEAT** Buckwheat is not really a wheat and is not even a cereal grain—it is in the rhubarb family. It has a hearty, earthy flavor that produces a moist, fine crumb and a soft crust. It is great in things like pancakes and is a good "mixer" with other flours. Nutritionally, it is high in all eight essential amino acids, calcium, B vitamins, and vitamin E. It takes a long time for the body to process buckwheat, making it a great stabilizer for blood sugar.

Buckwheat flour comes in light, medium, or dark grades, depending on how much of the black hull is ground up in the flour. You can make buckwheat flour in your own kitchen by grinding untoasted buckwheat groats in a blender or coffee grinder.

Some people do not like the taste and texture of things made with buckwheat flour, so start by substituting small amounts of buckwheat flour for wheat flour in recipes before going whole hog with your buckwheat. Even if you love the taste, don't overdo it. Rebecca Wood, author of *The New Whole Foods Encyclopedia* (1999), says "for a soft, aromatic cake or muffin with an earthy flavor, substitute 10 percent buckwheat flour for wheat flour. Add 30 percent or more buckwheat flour to bread and your loaf will have the density of a brick and the moistness of a pudding."

**CORNMEAL** Cornmeal is a staple for those of us who try to use as many farmers' market ingredients as we can in our baking. There are mills in communities across the country that grind corn into meal, and there are countless ways in which to use it. Cornmeal comes in white, yellow, and occasionally blue or red.

Yellow cornmeal, which is the most common, tastes the most like corn and produces a grainy texture. White cornmeal has a more delicate flavor, and blue or red cornmeal is sweeter with an almost nutty flavor. Blue corn is an open pollinated plant and has considerably more protein, iron, manganese, and potassium than the yellow or white varieties. All cornmeals are great in both sweet and savory dishes. Use it in cornbread (of course), tamales, polenta, muffins, crackers, waffles, pancakes, and some yeast breads.

Be sure to read the label before purchasing cornmeal. Look for stone ground or water ground whole cornmeal, not degerminated. Coarse-ground corn meal is great for some things, but is not so good for baking, as it retains a gritty consistency.

**GARBANZO FLOUR** This is also known as chickpea flour. With a sweet and rich flavor, it produces a dry, delicate crumb in baking. When baking traditional breads or flatbreads, it's a good idea to mix no more than 25 percent garbanzo flour with a gluten flour. Garbanzo flour is high in protein. Because it has a strong flavor, it is best used in recipes with other strongly flavored ingredients such as applesauce, cocoa, maple syrup, honey, or cinnamon.

Try it in muffins, cookies, and quick breads.

**MESQUITE FLOUR** This flour is made by grinding the ripened pods of the mesquite tree. It was a primary source of meal by Native Americans in the southwestern United States and in Mexico. It is high in protein and tastes somewhat like molasses. It is good in muffins, cakes, breads, and cookies when combined with other flours (gluten-free or wheat flour). Because it has a strong and distinct flavor, you might want to include only ¼ cup or less until you determine whether you (and your family) like the taste.

This flour is very sweet, so you might need to alter the amount of additional sweeteners you use in things baked with mesquite flour. If you like the taste but don't want to be overpowered by it, just use mesquite flour as a spice or flavoring rather than as a baking flour. This tastes particularly good in "south of the border" recipes such as flans or sweet breads. Because it contains a soluble fiber that takes a long time to digest, mesquite flour helps stabilize blood sugars. This is excellent for diabetics to use in combination with natural sweeteners that are low on the glycemic index, such as agave nectar.

**OAT FLOUR** There is some controversy about the gluten-free status of oats. The oats themselves are usually not the problem, but the machinery used for milling wheat is also used in processing oats, and is thus contaminated with gluten. Just be sure to buy your oats from a local source that does not use their machinery to grind wheat.

Oat flour is sweet and produces a moist, cakelike crumb when used in cakes, crackers, breads, and pancakes. Things baked with a large amount of oat flour tend to stay fresh and moist longer (making them great for baked goods you want to ship off to loved ones). At one time, oats were added to breads and other baked goods to help extend their shelf life.

You can make your own oat flour by grinding rolled oats in a blender or coffee grinder. One and a quarter cups of rolled oats produces one cup of oat flour.

**QUINOA FLOUR** This flour has a nutty, earthy flavor and produces a cakelike crumb in baked goods. You can grind your own flour from whole quinoa—three quarters cup quinoa will make one cup flour. Grind in a food processor or blender. Be sure to rinse and toast the quinoa before you grind it to remove the natural bitter taste that is on the kernels (actually a naturally occurring insecticide!). Quinoa contains lysine, making it a complete protein.

Try substituting small amounts (up to about a quarter the total amount of flour) in cakes, muffins, and quick breads.

RICE FLOUR Rice flour has long been the staple for gluten-free baking. Mixed with other ingredients, such as tapioca flour, xanthan gum, potato starch, and others, rice flour provides a wonderful alternative to wheat flour. Things baked with rice flour tend to have a bit of a sandy texture, but this can be greatly reduced with the right combination of ingredients. When baking with rice flour, it's generally best to add a small amount of xanthan gum to help the dough stick together. This allows the dough to have enough form and structure to allow room for the gas bubbles to form, aiding the rise and leavening of the dough. (Add 1½ teaspoons xanthan gum per 2 cups flour.)

Brown rice flour, as you would expect, is made from grinding whole brown rice and is more nutritious than white rice flour. For a lighter color and texture, use white rice flour or blend the two. Rice flour is perhaps most useful when used in combination with other flours, either to reduce the amount of gluten in a recipe or to make it completely gluten-free.

All rice flours go rancid easily and should be stored in the refrigerator or the freezer.

SORGHUM FLOUR With a light brown color and subtle flavor, sorghum probably tastes more like wheat than any other gluten-free flour. Mixed with other flours, such as garbanzo or tapioca, and with the addition of a small amount of xanthan gum (use at a rate of about ½ teaspoon per cup of sorghum flour), sorghum will form the basis of wonderfully flavored, smooth-textured piecrusts and breads.

TEFF FLOUR Teff flour is made from a kind of millet so small that the whole kernel is ground to make the flour. Although it is tasty in all kinds of different baked goods, it is most famous as an ingredient in an Ethiopian flatbread called injera. Both brown and white teff flour are available, with the former offering a molasses taste. Teff has a naturally occurring yeast associated with it and, for this reason, should not be used in yeasted breads. It's great to use in combination with other flours in cookies, muffins, piecrusts, and waffles.

## Butter and Oils

If you think "fat" and immediately feel either disgust or guilt, think again. Think instead of creamy, rich butter from a local dairy or smooth, flavorful olive oil. Fats perform a multitude of services in baking. According to Shirley O. Corriher's book *CookWise* (1997), "Fats leaven—bubbles in the fat help cakes rise. Fats tenderize—they coat flour proteins and prevent their joining to form gluten. Fats act as a spacer to hold thin layers of dough apart for flaky pastry. Fats influence the amount that cookies spread."

There are numerous kinds of fats available for baking. Some are solid at room temperature; of these, butter and coconut oil are the two that appear in recipes in this book. Other oils included in the recipes remain a liquid at room temperature.

Solid and liquid fats act differently in recipes and should not be substituted freely for one another. Even melted butter and oil react differently, even though they are both liquids, because butter contains milk solids that will set up when cooled. Whipped butter should not be substituted for stick butter, because it contains significantly more air.

Going into the pros and cons about various fats (trans and otherwise) and their effect on your health is not the purpose of this book. The subject is confusing and controversial, even for experts. What we do suggest is that you eat only fats that are whole foods. Margarine, in any form, under any name, is not a real food. A product such as Earth Balance is a vegan alternative to butter and is made from a combination of expeller-pressed oils—all real foods.

### Butter
We consider butter one of God's gifts to bakers. The best butter is sweet and unsalted. If your state allows the sale of raw butter, purchase it. Anywhere you live, get organic butter whenever possible. Good butter smells sweet. If it has an unpleasant odor, the butter has gone rancid and should not be used.

Butter contains 80 percent fat.

Pay attention to the temperature of the butter for various recipes. Pastry recipes generally call for a really cold butter, while cake recipes call for room temperature.

### Oils
The process of extracting oil from seeds and nuts varies tremendously throughout the industry. Though they are usually less expensive, oils that are heated and refined should be avoided, as heat degrades both the flavor and the nutritional content of the oil. Unfortunately, heat helps produce a greater quantity of oil and is the preferred method of extraction by most companies.

Expeller pressing is a chemical-free process of extracting oil. Cold pressing refers to an expeller-press process that occurs in an environment below 122°F. (The latter definition is based on European Union standards. The United States's oil labeling regulations are not as strict.)

Be diligent in finding unrefined oils whenever possible. According to Rebecca Wood, "refined fats are carcinogenic; they suppress the immune system; they cause gastric distress and irritated lungs and mucus membranes; and they speed aging."

There are many culinary oils available, extracted from nuts, seeds, and fruits. Most of these, unfortunately, are not considered very healthful. Canola oil is ubiquitous, appearing in an astounding number of products, but there is some controversy about the pros and cons of using it. This is discussed in more detail later. The Weston Price Foundation (a nonprofit organization dedicated to providing information about human health and nutrition) approves only of olive, sesame (expeller-pressed), flaxseed, coconut, palm, and palm kernel oils. Rebecca Wood suggests using hazelnut, sesame, or olive oils. According to Sally Fallon, author of *Nourishing Traditions* (1999), safflower, corn, sunflower, soybean, and cottonseed oils are not healthful oils, particularly after they have been heated, and should not be used in baking for that reason. She says that olive oil has withstood the test of time and is the safest vegetable oil to use. She also suggests using flaxseed oil or coconut oil in baking.

Unrefined oils can be stored at room temperature for up to two months. If you need to store them longer, place them in the refrigerator.

### General Guidelines for Using Butter and Oils

Many of the recipes in the book call for oils we do not completely approve of, but we respect each of our contributors and so we have presented their recipes as they sent them to us. However, we wanted to point this out and also to offer some suggestions for more healthful oils.

As always, we recommend using whole foods that are only minimally processed. When you can, use butter. When a recipe calls for oil, perhaps the best substitution would be a very lightly flavored olive oil. Other oils, such as sesame, hazelnut, or the palm oils can also be used, depending on the recipe and the blending of flavors. Experiment, see what works best for you—and your body.

CANOLA OIL Perhaps no other oil sparks as much controversy as canola oil. As noted above, some experts (especially the Weston Price Foundation and Sally Fallon) don't approve of its use. Fallon says that canola oil has a high sulfur content and goes rancid easily, making it a less desirable oil to use. Others, including highly regarded food specialists Marion Nestle and Margaret Wittenberg, don't voice these same objections.

Canola oil is made from a recently developed type of mustard rape. Rapeseed oil has been a part of traditional cooking for three thousand years, though the big difference is that the rapeseed oil was pressed fresh daily using simple presses, a much more healthful extraction method than the one used by today's machines. Because of the extraction method, we do not recommend the use of canola oil in natural baking.

FLAXSEED OIL This goes rancid very quickly, so be sure to refrigerate. Use in small quantities.

OLIVE OIL The most traditional of all oils, olive oil has been used for 2,500 years. Cold-pressed extra virgin is the healthiest for you, but it has a robust flavor that is not always suitable for baking. A good alternative is cold-pressed light tasting olive oil.

**SAFFLOWER, CORN, SUNFLOWER, SOYBEAN, AND COTTONSEED OILS** These oils are included as ingredients in some of the book's recipes, but as a general rule we do not recommend them for use in natural baking.

**SESAME OIL** This can be used safely for baking. However, it has a strong flavor, so be sure to use it sparingly. Rebecca Wood suggests that it is best for use at oven temperatures below 325°F.

**TROPICAL OILS (COCONUT, PALM, AND PALM KERNEL)** These can be used in baking, especially coconut oil, which remains solid at room temperature and can be stored at room temperature for several months.

## Dairy

Some of the terms used in association with dairy products are not always clearly understood. Understanding these terms may aid in your dairy selections.

Nearly all of us grew up drinking homogenized milk without ever stopping to wonder what exactly that meant. The answer is pretty simple: Milk is comprised of drops of fat suspended in water. Since fat is lighter than water, it tends to rise to the top. Homogenization is the process of mechanically mixing it hard enough to break up the fat into minuscule droplets that remain blended.

There is a debate raging about the necessity and benefits of pasteurizing milk. Pasteurization is a process in which the milk is heated to a temperature high enough to kill most of the bacteria in it. Many people prefer the taste of unpasteurized milk. This is a personal preference, although many states do not allow the sale of unpasteurized milk.

Whatever you choose, though, whenever possible, purchase organic dairy products that are free of antibiotics and hormones.

Goat's milk is a good alternative for people who cannot tolerate the proteins in cow's milk.

## Eggs

*Cage free* means the hens are not confined to wire cages. *Free range* means they have access to the outdoors. *Pastured* means the chickens were raised on pastureland, with full access to sun, grass, and their traditional diet of insects, supplemented with grains and other feed. Pastured eggs are generally considered to be the most healthful type of eggs. *Organic* means the chickens are fed only organic vegetable feed, are cage free, and are not injected with antibiotics. Organic, free range, and pastured eggs are generally much more expensive than cage free. *Vegetarian* means the chickens are not fed meat products (most commercial feeds contain animal products and fish meal).

# Stocking the Pantry

SOME OF THE INGREDIENTS USED IN THESE RECIPES MAY, AT FIRST, SEEM A little odd to you, though they'll quickly become trusted friends. Before you start doing a lot of natural baking, we suggest that you stock your pantry with the things you'll need most often. There is nothing more frustrating than starting a recipe, only to realize that you need a quarter teaspoon of something that is not on your shelf. In this book, we have tried to limit the number of exotic, expensive ingredients that you need only occasionally in minute quantities, but we do still include the things that give each recipe unique, complex flavors. We've also tried to include substitutions for ingredients that may be hard to find.

As you read through the recipes, you'll notice we're big on substitutions and we offer suggestions to make these recipes work for your unique needs. We're not "cookie cutter" bakers, so to speak. Even if you use the exact ingredients called for in the basic recipe, the results will probably slightly vary a little each time you bake it. Because we use natural products, the recipes will differ from one season to another and even from one week to the next as the vagaries of weather and climate play their part in forming the harvest. It is part of the delight of using real foods—they are a little unpredictable, but always delicious!

· · · · · · ·

The vast majority of these ingredients can be found at farmers' markets or food stores that carry whole, more nutritious foods and products. If you live in a community that does not yet have such a store, talk to your local supermarket manager and see if he or she will order these products for you (and for the growing number of people who love to bake naturally). Of course you can get almost anything online these days, and we have included a good list of Internet suppliers in the Resources section of the Appendix.

If you bake a lot, you might choose to buy in bulk quantities. This not only saves time and energy on your part, but also reduces your environmental impact. Buying large quantities saves in packaging materials and in shipping (and thus fuel) costs as well as reducing your trips to the market. Be aware, though, that many products, including some of the flours and grains, have a relatively short shelf life. For example, rice flour has natural oils in it that are prone to go rancid easily, so it should be stored in the refrigerator or freezer or used right away. In general, you can keep rice flour in the refrigerator for four to five months or in the freezer for up to a year when stored in a sealed container or tightly wrapped, but check it often for an unpleasant odor. This, of course, is an indicator that it has gone rancid and should not be used.

When you can, buy fair trade items. Items marked as fair trade are from companies that produce their goods in a way that offers fair compensation to their workers and adheres to both a social and environmental standard. The most common fair trade products are not local products, but include things such as coffee, cocoa, tea, bananas, honey, and wine. Look for a FAIR TRADE label on the things you buy.

If you're serious about altering the way you bake, go ahead and invest in the basic pantry ingredients that are found in many of these recipes. The ingredients found in the list to the right are prioritized, with the most commonly used items listed first and the less frequently used items listed last. For example, when it comes to sweeteners, we use a lot more honey than date sugar crystals.

## Basic Pantry Ingredients

### Flours and Grains
Whole wheat pastry flour, all-purpose unbleached flour, rolled oats, stone-ground cornmeal, whole wheat flour, whole-grain spelt flour, rice flour (brown and white), brown rice, buckwheat, quinoa

### Non-local Goods
Grain-sweetened chocolate chips, unsweetened chocolate (bars and cocoa powder), cinnamon (and other spices), vanilla, baking soda, baking powder (aluminum-free), sea salt

### Dairy
Fresh produce and dairy products including eggs, cheeses, butter, and milk will have to be bought fresh regularly

### Nuts and Seeds
Walnuts, pecans, almonds, peanut butter (unsweetened), sunflower seeds, sesame seeds, coconut, pine nuts, pumpkin seeds

### Oils
Olive oil, coconut oil, palm oil, palm kernel oil, walnut oil, sesame oil, almond oil

### Sweeteners
Honey (local), maple syrup, agave nectar, brown rice syrup, barley malt syrup, maple sugar, date sugar crystals

# Substitutions

SUBSTITUTING WHOLESOME INGREDIENTS FOR LESS HEALTHFUL ONES can be challenging when baking sweets. After all, we've been raised to believe that sugar and white flour are essential ingredients for most desserts. But, as evidenced by the terrific recipes we collected for this book, with a few tips and ideas, using locally grown ingredients and natural sweeteners in baking can be done, and done well.

If you've had less-than-spectacular experiences in your attempts to substitute more healthful ingredients for refined sugar and white flour, then you have a treat in store—actually one hundred treats—because every recipe in this book has been tested and retested to make sure that it is, above all, delicious.

• • • • • • •

## Substituting for Refined Sugar

Although it's relatively easy to substitute whole grains for white flour (with a few important tips, which you'll see later in this section), it is admittedly more challenging to substitute liquids such as maple syrup and honey for a dry ingredient such as sugar. The volume is different, the flour absorbs the liquid in a different way, and the chemical mixture is simply not the same. However, inspired by the importance of baking with local whole foods and using less sugar in our diets, chefs and bakers have become more interested in altering traditional recipes to include natural sweeteners in place of sugar.

### Sugar Substitutes

We do not use any sugar products in our recipes. This includes brown sugar, molasses, demerara, turbinado, muscovado, cane syrup, or evaporated cane syrup. We do this, in part, for dietary reasons. We firmly believe that sugar in any form is detrimental to our health and that of our family. We also do this to help support the small producers of alternative sweeteners—the honeybee keepers, the maple syrup farmers, and so on. You may not choose to be as "pure" as we are, but the results we've experienced from avoiding sugar products are pretty exciting and delicious.

Each natural sweetener has a unique personality and each one varies from the others (and from sugar) in weight, moisture, acidity, relative sweetness, and, of course, taste. Take weight as an example: While a cup of sugar weighs 8 ounces, both honey and maple syrup are denser and heavier by volume—a cup of maple syrup weighs 11 ounces and a cup of honey weighs 12 ounces. Not surprisingly, we found that when substituting natural sweeteners, some recipes were easier to alter than others. When gathering recipes for this book, one contributor generously offered to let us modify one of her prize-winning cake recipes. I was very excited until I saw that the first ingredient listed was 3 cups of sugar! It's virtually impossible to substitute for this volume of sugar. You would end up with something completely different from the original.

On the other hand, things like pie filling and sauces that are good when they're kind of syrupy and gooey anyway, were easy to modify because we were dealing only with differences in taste and sweetness, not texture and consistency.

Two books became our bibles for altering recipes: Shirley O. Corriher's *CookWise* (1997) and Cook's Illustrated *The New Best Recipe* (2004). I highly recommend both of them. They go into the "why" of baking, and explain how different recipes change with different amounts of ingredients. Neither book addresses the issue of substituting natural sweeteners for dry sugar, but they did offer enough information about fats, grains, eggs, and such to make experimenting a lot of fun.

## General Rules

The following chart provides the basics for substituting natural sweeteners for white or brown sugar. The general rule for substituting is to decrease the other liquids called for in the recipe and add a little more baking soda. Since some natural sweeteners (maple syrup, agave nectar, and honey) are sweeter than sugar, you will use a smaller amount than the sugar called for in the original recipe. Barley malt and brown rice syrups are not as sweet, so in those cases you'll use slightly more. Dry date sugar and maple sugar can be substituted one for one.

We really liked the results we got when we combined sweeteners. For example, mixing a thicker, less sweet syrup (such as barley malt or brown rice) with a thinner one (such as maple or agave nectar) helps balance out the volume problem and the difference in sweetness. Since you need slightly less of the thinner liquid and slightly more of the thicker liquid, combining the two allows you to substitute almost equally for one cup of sugar.

Of course, there are exceptions. In the Green Market Baking Book Yellow Layer

# Substitution Chart
## For each cup of sugar:

| Natural sweetener | Amount to Use | Liquid Removed | Additional Baking Soda | Notes |
|---|---|---|---|---|
| **Maple syrup** | ⅔–¾ cup | 3 tablespoons | +¼ teaspoon | Grade B creates richer flavor |
| Maple sugar | 1 cup | none | +⅛ teaspoon | Sift before adding |
| **Agave nectar** | ¾ cup | –⅓ cup | none | Reduce temperature by 25°F |
| Barley malt syrup | 1⅓ cup | –¼ cup | +¼ teaspoon | Use with other sweetener |
| **Brown rice syrup** | 1⅓ cup | –¼ cup | +¼ teaspoon | Use with other sweetener |
| Honey | ¾–1 cup | –¼ cup | +¼ teaspoon | Reduce temperature 25°F |
| **Date sugar** | 1 cup | none | none | Use with other sweetener |

There are challenges to using the above chart. For example, many recipes (such as most cookie recipes) don't call for any liquid, so there's nothing to reduce. Many people will advise that if no liquid is called for, the amount of flour should be increased, but we found that didn't work very well. Adding flour often made baked goods dense and tough and diluted the flavors of the other ingredients. We typically adjusted the amount of ingredients such as butter and eggs, instead.

*Different sweeteners can be combined with spectacular results. Try:*

- ½ cup maple syrup plus ½ cup brown rice syrup for 1 cup sugar
- ½ cup agave nectar plus ½ cup barley malt syrup for 1 cup sugar
- ¾ cup maple syrup plus ¼ cup barley malt syrup for 1 cup sugar

Cake recipe that follows, we use only honey, which adds a simple sweetness rather than a complex flavor. For a complete discussion of the different sweeteners and suggestions for how to use them, see pages 11–15.

It's sometimes easier to grasp a concept when you see it put into practice, so we've included two recipes here, for chocolate chip cookies and a yellow layer cake. We've listed the traditional recipes and then shown how we altered them to substitute for the refined sugar.

## Sugar Substitutions in Cookies

One of the biggest recipe challenges we faced in writing this book was making a traditional-style chocolate chip cookie recipe without sugar. (For weeks, my husband came home from work to a kitchen full of diverse chocolate chip cookies. Fortunately, he has a high metabolism and was able to taste and critique nightly without gaining weight!) It's the sugar that makes a chocolate chip cookie melt and spread and recrystallize into that yummy, caramel-flavored crisp cookie. Unfortunately, ingredients such as honey

and maple syrup tend to retain moisture, which prevents spreading and makes for a more cakelike cookie.

We learned a lot by making this recipe over and over. We discovered that butter helps make a cookie spread, that egg whites tend to dry out batter, and that a low-protein flour (such as cake flour) makes a cookie puff up, but a high-protein flour (such as bread flour) makes it tough. We also learned that to help make a cookie spread, the ingredients should be at room temperature and that the oven should be at a slightly lower temperature so the cookie bakes a little longer. As you would suspect, a thinner batter makes for a thinner cookie.

The solution to this cookie challenge turned out to be a little expensive: maple sugar. But this is one recipe for which we definitely think it's worth spending the extra money. You simply have to have the crystals to get the crisp. We combined it with (slightly less expensive) maple syrup and then experimented with different ingredients and amounts, altered the time of baking and the temperature and everything else we could think of, and came up with a great version of a traditional chocolate chip cookie. We've listed both recipes here so you can see the differences.

# TRADITIONAL CHOCOLATE CHIP COOKIES

1 cup butter

¾ cup sugar

¾ cup packed brown sugar

1 large egg

1 teaspoon vanilla extract

2¼ cups all-purpose flour

1 teaspoon baking soda

½ teaspoon salt

2 cups semisweet chocolate chips

1 cup chopped pecans (optional)

**1.** Preheat the oven to 350°F.

**2.** In a large mixing bowl, cream the butter until fluffy, then add the sugars.

**3.** Add the egg and vanilla and beat well.

**4.** In a separate bowl, mix together the flour, baking soda, and salt.

**5.** Gradually add this to the butter mixture.

**6.** Fold in the chocolate chips and pecans (if desired).

**7.** Drop by spoonfuls onto a greased or parchment paper-lined cookie sheet. Bake for 10–12 minutes, until brown around edges. Do not overbake.

**8.** Remove the cookies from the baking sheet and cool on a wire rack.

# GREEN MARKET BAKING BOOK
# CHOCOLATE CHIP COOKIES

1 cup maple sugar

1½ cups (3 sticks) organic butter, at room temperature

½ cup maple syrup

1 egg yolk

1 teaspoon vanilla extract

2 cups all-purpose flour

1¼ teaspoons baking soda

½ teaspoon salt

1 cup grain-sweetened chocolate chips (see Resources)

1 cup chopped pecans or walnuts (optional)

**1.** Preheat the oven to 325°F.

**2.** Use a coffee grinder or a food processor to grind the maple sugar until superfine.

**3.** Mix the butter with the maple sugar and blend until smooth. Add the maple syrup and blend well.

**4.** Add the egg yolk, then the vanilla. Mix well.

**5.** In a large bowl, mix the flour with the baking soda and salt.

**6.** Blend the flour mixture into the butter mixture, mixing it well.

**7.** Fold in the chocolate chips and nuts.

**8.** Grease a cookie sheet or line it with parchment paper. Drop the batter by large spoonfuls onto the cookie sheet. Flatten the batter slightly with the bottom of a glass or palm of your hand.

**9.** Bake 11–13 minutes, until brown around the edges. Do not overbake.

**10.** Remove the pan from the oven and allow the cookies to cool about 2 minutes, then transfer them to a wire rack to finish cooling.

**Note:** *If you leave these to cool on a plate instead of a rack, they will not be as crisp.*

## Sugar Substitutions in Cakes

Substituting natural sweeteners for sugar is easier to do in cakes than in cookies. Here, we've offered a yellow layer cake and shown you how we have altered it.

# TRADITIONAL YELLOW LAYER CAKE

1½ cups (3 sticks) butter, at room temperature

2 cups sugar

4 eggs

3 cups all-purpose flour

3 teaspoons baking powder

1 teaspoon salt

1 cup milk

1 teaspoon vanilla extract

**1.** Preheat the oven to 350°F. Grease and flour three 9-inch round pans.

**2.** Blend the butter and sugar until fluffy.

**3.** Add the eggs, one at a time.

**4.** In a separate bowl, sift the flour, baking powder, and salt together.

**5.** Combine the milk and vanilla.

**6.** Alternately add the dry ingredients and the milk mixture to the egg mixture, ending with the dry ingredients. Do not overmix. Pour the mixture into pans.

**7.** Bake for 20–25 minutes, until the top of the cake springs back when touched or a toothpick inserted into the center of the cake comes out clean.

# GREEN MARKET BAKING BOOK
## YELLOW LAYER CAKE

1½ cups (3 sticks) butter, at room temperature

1¾ cups honey

4 eggs

1 cup whole wheat pastry flour

2 cups minus 1 tablespoon all-purpose flour

1 tablespoon arrowroot

2½ teaspoons baking powder

½ teaspoon baking soda

1 teaspoon salt

¾ cup milk

1 teaspoon vanilla extract

**1.** Preheat the oven to 325°F. Grease and flour three 9-inch round pans.

**2.** Beat together the butter and honey.

**3.** Add the eggs, one at a time.

**4.** In a separate bowl, sift together the flours, arrowroot, baking powder, baking soda, and salt.

**5.** Combine the milk and vanilla.

**6.** Alternately add the dry ingredients and the milk mixture to the egg mixture, ending with the dry ingredients. Pour the mixture into pans.

**7.** Bake for 30–35 minutes, until the top of the cake springs back when touched or a toothpick inserted into the center of the cake comes out clean.

**Note:** *Arrowroot helps lighten the batter of this cake. This is a fabulous cake to use as a base for Baked Alaska (pages 158–159) or English Fruit Trifle (page 79), or as a layer cake for special occasions. Check the index for a variety of icing possibilities. Serve with Maple Ice Cream (page 149) or Blueberry Ginger Sauce (page 107).*

## Sugar Substitutions in Chocolate Cake

Using cocoa powder instead of bar chocolate helps balance out the volume and texture of chocolate cakes made with natural sweeteners. Otherwise, substituting in a chocolate cake is similar to substituting in a yellow cake. In general, for every ounce of chocolate, substitute 3 tablespoons of cocoa powder, add an extra 1 tablespoon of oil or butter, reduce the amount of liquid by about one-quarter for every cup of liquid in the traditional recipe, add ¼ teaspoon more baking soda per cup of flour, and bake at a slightly cooler temperature (approximately 25°F lower) for a little longer (about five to ten minutes, but watch it carefully so it doesn't burn).

## Sugar Substitutions in Pie Filling

Most fruit pies lend themselves beautifully to substitution. Simply substitute maple syrup or honey for the sugar. It works well if you cook the fruit filling before putting it in the pie shell. If it looks too runny, cook it down until some of the liquid has evaporated. Don't overcook it—the fruit will become mushy. Alternatively, you can add a tablespoon of arrowroot to the filling to thicken it. For custard-type pie fillings, use slightly more arrowroot to thicken.

## Substituting for Flour

When we're baking, we avoid using bleached white flour since the bleaching process involves using chemicals, although some of the recipes here do call for unbleached white flour. After reading this section, however, you should be able to substitute flours as you see fit. It's relatively easy to substitute whole-grain flours for at least part of the white flour called for in a recipe. But, just like substituting for sugar, substituting for wheat flour can be a little confusing. Gluten-free flours do not act like those with gluten but, with a little work and know-how, they can be equally delicious. As a general rule, we didn't bother with sifting any of the flours that we used.

## Substituting for White Flour

If you use all whole wheat flour as a substitute for white flour, the texture of your baked goods will be very dense. Debra Lynn Dadd, diva of healthful cooking, suggests that for every cup of whole wheat flour that you substitute for white flour, you take out one tablespoon of flour and put in one tablespoon of arrowroot to help lighten the recipe. Whole wheat pastry flour (which produces a lighter dough than a regular whole wheat) and white whole wheat flour are both great substitutes to use in a variety of recipes. For a complete listing of different flours and their uses, see pages 15–20.

If you are baking something that you want to be light and airy, such as the Yellow Layer Cake (page 33) or Martha Foose's Maple Sugar Angel Food Cake (page 157), you're probably going to want to use unbleached all-purpose flour.

## Substituting for Wheat-Based Flours

Gluten is an elastic protein found in many grains and flours, including wheat and rye. Some people are sensitive to gluten, and many people suffer from an inability to digest gluten altogether (a condition called celiac disease). Wheat is incredibly prevalent in so much of what we eat that many people suffer from at least a little bit of wheat and gluten overdose.

If you have issues with gluten, be diligent in finding products that are truly gluten-free, because gluten appears in unexpected places. For example, research indicates that although oats do not contain gluten, they are commercially processed in machines that also process wheat and, therefore, are often contaminated with traces of gluten.

In addition to being found in breads and baked goods, gluten is also found in pasta, cereals, crackers, beer, some chocolate milk, some brown rice syrup, and many, many other products. Since many of the recipes in this book call for brown rice syrup, be sure you check to make sure the ones you use are gluten-free if this is an issue for you.

For those with gluten intolerance, there are many possible substitutions for baking everything you want to eat. Substituting a nongluten flour for wheat is the quick answer. Nongluten flours include rice (brown and white), tapioca, corn, soy, pecan meal, almond meal, and garbanzo, among others. Most experts think that amaranth, quinoa, buckwheat, and millet are also gluten-free, though some controversy remains. For a list of nongluten flours, see pages 17–20.

Fortunately, a lot of research has been done on gluten-free baking, and there are excellent commercially available gluten-free mixes for everything from pancakes to cookies and bread to piecrusts. Be sure to read the list of ingredients before using these products, though, so you don't inadvertently include something else you are allergic to (such as nuts) or are philosophically opposed to (such as dairy).

There are also several make-it-yourself formulas for replacing wheat flour with gluten-free ingredients. As you've probably noticed, we're a "from scratch" crowd. Here are a couple of our favorite made-from-scratch gluten-free baking mixes:

For every cup of wheat flour (brown, white, or unbleached) use:

- ¼ cup soy flour
- ¼ cup tapioca flour
- ½ cup brown rice flour
- 2 teaspoons xanthan gum

Or use a combination of the following (in equal amounts):

- Rice flour (white, brown, or a combination of the two)
- Sorghum flour
- Garbanzo flour

Mix until you have an amount equal to what is called for in the recipe, then add 2 teaspoons xanthan gum per cup. Xanthan gum is a naturally occurring inactive bacterium that is treated and processed to make a thickening and stabilizing agent. It is particularly useful in gluten-free baking because it acts as a binding agent, giving the dough or batter the necessary viscosity that is normally provided by the gluten.

Or, make up this large batch, blend it together, and substitute it for wheat flour at a one-to-one ratio.

- 6 cups white rice flour
- 2 cups potato starch
- 1 cup tapioca flour
- 5 teaspoons xanthan gum

**Note:** *Because of the ongoing uncertainty over what contains gluten (particularly in the case of oats), we've designated our recipes wheat-free rather than gluten-free.*

## Other Substitutions

Each of us has our own food issues. Some of these issues are prompted by allergies or dietary needs, others by environmental, social, or humanitarian concerns. From locavore to omnivore, from vegan to fair trade advocate, each of us regards food a little differently. We can't cover all these issues in this book as thoroughly as the subjects warrant, but we can offer hints and tips that have worked well for us.

The recipes in this book that address particular needs (such as dairy-free, vegan, and wheat-free recipes) are marked as such in the recipe title.

**Note:** *Some vegans avoid the use of honey. For the purposes of this book, we do include honey in our vegan recipes.*

### Egg Substitutions

Eggs help bind the other ingredients together and also leaven the batter. When only one egg is called for in a recipe, it is possible to substitute any of the following, adding baking powder as noted. When a recipe calls for more than three eggs, in all likelihood, it will be necessary to use real eggs.

For every egg in a recipe, you can substitute the following:

- ½ mashed banana
- ¼ cup soft tofu (for fewer calories)
- Ener-G (a commercial product made from vegetable starch)
- ¼ cup applesauce, pumpkin (canned or fresh), or pureed prunes (with ½ tsp baking powder to lighten the batter)
- 1 tablespoon soy or bean flour (such as garbanzo flour), with 1 tablespoon water
- 2 tablespoons cornstarch and 2 tablespoons water
- 1 tablespoon ground flaxseed and ¼ cup water

### Cow's Milk Substitutions

*Substitute any of the following at a one-to-one ratio. Almond milk has a distinct flavor, so using it in some recipes will be a definite asset.*

Soy milk

Almond milk

Rice milk

### Butter Substitutions

Butter and oils do not act exactly the same in a recipe. A solid fat, such as butter, contains milk solids that set when cooled and that hold air bubbles, giving more "lift" to your batter. A liquid fat (for example, most oils) does not set, creating a denser product. Taking these differences into consideration, oil remains a good substitute for butter in many recipes.

In general, using oil instead of butter results in cakelike cookies and dense, moist cakes. To substitute oil for butter, reduce the amount of oil by 25 percent. For example, for ½ cup (1 stick) of butter, use ½ cup minus 2 tablespoons of oil. For 1 cup (two sticks) of butter, use ¾ cup of oil. All Earth Balance natural butter substitutes can be substituted at a one-to-one ratio.

Try the following when substituting for butter:

- Very lightly flavored oil, such as an extra light olive oil
- Tropical oils—coconut, flax, palm, and palm kernel
- Earth Balance spread

## Substituting to Lower Fats and Reduce Calories

We believe in eating whole foods and not dividing them up into parts or units, including calories. We also believe that if you have issues with your weight, it's better to choose foods that are naturally low in calories rather than trying to substitute commercially available low-fat products for ingredients in these recipes.

You might have noticed that many of these recipes call for a considerable amount of butter. We think butter is one of the earth's best foods, and it seems to make almost everything taste better. Unfortunately, butter is composed primarily of pure fat, so if you're watching your fat intake, you'll have to be moderate in how much of it you eat. There are several recipes included, such as Apple Pecan Drops from Schermer Pecans, and Melanie Waxman's Beautiful Brown Rice Pudding, that are naturally low in calories and that are fabulous, wonderful, and delicious.

If you're watching your caloric intake, be conscious of extra calories that can pile up in a recipe. For example, many of these recipes call for nuts, which are sometimes an essential part of the recipe, but at other times can easily be left out. The pecans in the Green Market Bakers' Oatmeal Raisin Cookies are delicious, but the cookies are just as good without them, so eliminating them from the recipe would help reduce the number of calories per cookie. However, the ground almonds in Meredith McCarty's Toasted Almond and Orange Cake with Orange Glaze are absolutely necessary for the recipe to work.

Of course there are some whole foods that are (thankfully) naturally low in calories that can be easily substituted for higher-fat, higher-calorie ones. Try the following:

- Substitute up to half the fat (butter or oil) with applesauce or prune puree. (For example, if the recipe calls for ½ cup butter, use ¼ cup butter and ¼ cup prune puree.)
- Substitute naturally low-fat plain yogurt (especially the wonderfully thick Greek yogurt) for sour cream in cakes, bar cookies, quick breads, or muffins.
- Substitute 2 egg whites for a whole egg.

Apricots
Asparagus
Beets
Broccoli
Carrots
Cauliflower
Chives
Fennel
Green onions
Leeks
Mushrooms
New potatoes
Parsley
Rhubarb
Rosemary
Spinach
Strawberries
Vidalia onions

# SPRING

THE OTHER DAY I WATCHED MY SMALL GRANDSON SITTING IN THE WARM spring sunshine eating bite after tiny bite of fresh, organic strawberries, a wide smile across his face. I understand how he felt! As I dive headfirst into spring, I, too, wear a wide smile. I'm happy to exchange a sweater for a T-shirt, glad to slip off heavy shoes and feel the warming earth beneath my toes. For a while, it's enough just to sit in the sunshine, but, as always, my thoughts eventually turn to food and to what the season has to offer.

Perhaps nothing announces the arrival of this new season better than bright red strawberries polka-dotted with seeds. Strawberries grow almost everywhere, and the fresher they are, the better they taste. Though they are fabulous all by themselves, they are even better slipped between layers of buttermilk shortcake and topped with Honey-Sweetened Whipped Cream (page 49) in one of the best strawberry shortcake recipes I've ever tasted.

Our recipe contributors have come up with some unusual and delicious ways to use these spring berries. Try the Honey Strawberry Shortcakes (pages 48–49) or Christina Pirello's Sweet Strawberry Pie (page 54).

The sweetness of the season can be found in other foods as well. Blushing apricots, tender asparagus, pungent herbs, earthy mushrooms, and crisp rhubarb are all signs that winter has gone for another year and that the spring season of harvest is upon us. And some of this produce is being used in some unexpected ways. For a darkly decadent (and unusual) cake, try Farmer John's Chocolate Beet Cake (pages 46–47)—there's really nothing quite like it. Or try Molly Stevens's Asparagus-Ricotta Tart with Comté Cheese (page 60) for a special Sunday brunch. Include one of Chef Ann Cooper's super-delicious and super-healthful muffins (pages 57–59) on the menu and your guests will rave.

If your market has an abundance of spring carrots, try using them in the Spring Carrot Teacakes with Maple Cream Cheese Frosting (page 44) or Susan Baldassano's absolutely delicious Carrot Halva Pudding (page 53).

Whatever you choose to make (and we hope you'll try them all), you'll find that the freshest offerings of spring are the perfect ingredients for the most delicious things you'll ever bake!

• • • • • • •

## Choosing Produce

**APRICOTS** Choose apricots that are firm and plump and that give a little when pressed with your thumb. Avoid fruit that is bruised or blemished. Do not buy under-ripe fruit, since it will not continue to ripen after it's picked. Stored in the refrigerator, fresh apricots should last a week or longer. To peel, put in boiling water for 45 to 60 seconds, then immediately plunge into ice water. The peel will slide right off.

**ARUGULA** Choose bright green, crisp leaves with no brown or soggy spots on them. Clean thoroughly, then dry and store in a plastic container in the refrigerator for several days.

**ASPARAGUS** Choose firm, straight stalks with compact, pointed tips. With asparagus, thick is better than thin. Avoid wilted or deformed stalks. Chill the asparagus stalks as quickly as you can and use them as soon as possible. If you need to store them in the refrigerator, wrap the stalk ends (not the tips!) in a damp paper towel and place in a plastic container in the refrigerator. Alternatively, place the stalk ends in a small glass of water in the fridge.

**BEETS** Buy small- to medium-sized beets that are smooth with no splits. Try to find beets with the greens still on, as these are usually fresher (you can also eat the greens on really young beets). To store, remove the tops (but do not wash) and place in plastic containers. They will last a week or more in the refrigerator. When you're ready to use them, scrub them well but don't peel them.

**CARROTS** Select smooth, firm carrots, avoiding those that are flabby or cracked or that have a green tinge on the carrot itself. Remove the leafy tops before storing, then put the carrots in a plastic container in the refrigerator. Do not store carrots with apples or other fruits that emit volatile gases while ripening. Small carrots, or larger ones cut into pieces, freeze well. You can even freeze grated carrots. Measure them into quantities used in baking (i.e., 1 cup or 1½ cups), place in freezer bags, and store them in the freezer until you're ready to use them.

**FENNEL** Fennel tastes like a combination of celery, licorice, and leeks and is widely used in Mediterranean cuisine. Fennel can be eaten from top to bottom as all parts are useful, from the bulb to the leaves and stalks to the seeds. Select bulbs that are clean and firm, with no spotting or discoloration. The bulb should be pale green, and the stalk and leaves should be bright green without signs of wilting. Flowers on the stalk indicate that the plant is past prime and should not be chosen. Store the unwashed bulb and leaves wrapped in plastic in the crisper drawer of the refrigerator. When you're ready to use it, wash the plant, cut the bulb off the stalk, cut the base off the bulb, then cut it in half vertically and remove the hard core.

*Some fruits and vegetables emit ethylene gas as they ripen (harmless in the amounts emitted by most produce). This gas accelerates the ripening of other fruits and vegetables stored in the same place.*

### Produce that emits ethylene

Apples

Avocados

Bananas

Melons

Mushrooms

Peaches

Pears

Plums

Tomatoes

### Produce that absorbs ethylene

Beans

Carrots

Cucumbers

Eggplant

Leafy Greens

Peas

Peppers

Potatoes

**LEEKS** Choose leeks that are firm and straight, but not too large. Leeks that are less than one and a half inches in diameter will be more tender than the larger ones. You can keep fresh leeks up to two weeks in the crisper drawer of the refrigerator, but once cooked they perish quickly. To prepare, cut off the dark green portions, then slice the white part of the leek in half lengthwise. Rinse under running water to remove the dirt.

**NEW POTATOES** Choose small, firm potatoes with smooth skin, free of green sprouts. Store them in a paper bag in a cool place (a pantry or cellar) for up to five days. If necessary, put in the crisper drawer of the refrigerator.

**RHUBARB** Choose fresh, crisp stalks. If you don't need to use rhubarb immediately, put it in a plastic container and store it in the crisper drawer of the refrigerator. When you are ready to use it, peel off any stringy covering, discard the leaves, and trim the ends. Rhubarb freezes well.

**SCALLIONS** Choose bright green tops and firm white bases. Leave these unwashed and wrapped in plastic for up to five days. Before using, wash scallions and trim off roots.

**SPINACH** Choose dark green leaves with no blemishes. Clean thoroughly, then dry and store in a plastic container in the refrigerator for several days.

# SPRING CARROT TEACAKES
## WITH MAPLE CREAM CHEESE FROSTING

### TEACAKES

4 eggs

1 cup maple syrup (preferably Grade B)

1¼ cups light olive oil

½ cup sour cream

1 tablespoon lemon juice

2 teaspoons vanilla extract

1 cup spelt flour

1 cup unbleached all-purpose flour

½ teaspoon salt

1 tablespoon baking powder

2 teaspoons cinnamon

3 cups grated carrots

1 cup chopped nuts, such as walnuts or pecans

### FROSTING

12 ounces cream cheese, softened

¼ cup maple syrup

1 teaspoon vanilla extract

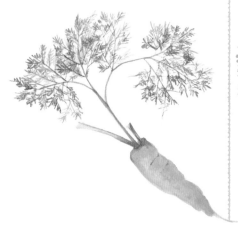

**Makes 12**

*A beautiful version of an old favorite, these carrot teacakes make a great little morsel to serve at a spring party—or just as an after-dinner delight for the family. The spelt flour offers a nutty, wholesome flavor without being heavy. These are great even without the Maple Cream Cheese Frosting (but even more delicious with it)!—GMB*

**1.** Preheat the oven to 325°F.

**2.** Beat the eggs until frothy. In a separate bowl, mix the maple syrup, oil, sour cream, lemon juice, and vanilla extract. Add the syrup mixture to the eggs and beat another minute.

**3.** Sift the flour, salt, baking powder, and cinnamon. Add to the egg mixture and mix until just combined.

**4.** Fold in the carrots and nuts.

**5.** Pour into cupcake liners in a muffin pan and bake for 20 minutes, or until a toothpick inserted in the center comes out clean. Top with Maple Cream Cheese Frosting.

### MAPLE CREAM CHEESE FROSTING

**1.** Beat ingredients together until fluffy and spreadable. Use a generous dollop on top of each Spring Carrot Teacake.

**GMB Tip:** *For a smoother, lighter texture, omit the spelt flour and use an all-purpose flour.*

# HONEY WHOLE WHEAT GINGER SPICE CAKE

2⅓ cups whole wheat pastry flour

1½ teaspoons baking powder

½ teaspoon baking soda

1 teaspoon ground ginger

1 teaspoon ground cinnamon

½ teaspoon ground cloves

½ teaspoon salt

¾ cup (1½ sticks) unsalted butter, at room temperature

1 cup clover honey

3 large egg yolks

⅞ cup plain yogurt

4 large egg whites

## Debra Lynn Dadd

**Makes one 9-inch tube cake, one Bundt cake, or two rounds**

*This cake has an amazingly light texture for a whole-grain cake. It is delicious warm right out of the pan, or it could be served with a little glaze or with fruit and whipped cream.—Debra*

**1.** Preheat the oven to 350°F. Grease and flour the pan(s).

**2.** In a large bowl, whisk together the flour, baking powder, baking soda, ginger, cinnamon, cloves, and salt.

**3.** In the bowl of an electric mixer, cream the butter on high speed. Gradually add the honey and beat on high speed for about 2 minutes.

**4.** Add the egg yolks, one at a time, beating into the mixture after each one.

**5.** With the mixer on low, add the flour mixture in three parts, alternating with the yogurt in two parts. Beat until the mixture is smooth, scraping down the sides of the bowl as necessary.

**6.** In another large bowl, beat the egg whites until stiff peaks form.

**7.** Fold the egg whites into the batter.

**8.** Pour the batter into the prepared pan(s) and bake 45 to 55 minutes, or until a toothpick inserted into the center comes out clean.

**9.** Let the cake cool in the pan on a wire rack. Cut and serve.

**GMB Tip:** *We found this to be a perfect base for maple vanilla poached pears. You can also make a glaze from maple syrup, butter, and cream (see Apple Cake recipe, page 116).*

# CHOCOLATE BEET CAKE

3 medium beets

1 cup light olive oil, plus
  extra for coating the pan

¾ cup maple syrup*

¾ cup mild-flavored honey,
  such as clover or orange
  blossom*

3 eggs

1 teaspoon vanilla extract

2 cups all-purpose flour,
  plus extra for dusting
  the pan

¾ cup cocoa powder**

2 teaspoons baking soda

⅓ teaspoon salt

* original recipe called for 1¾
  cups white sugar instead of
  maple syrup and honey

** original recipe called for
  4 ounces unsweetened
  chocolate instead of cocoa
  powder

**GMB Tip:** *Wow! What a
cake—beets never tasted so
good! Be prepared, though;
after you make the batter,
everything in your kitchen
is going to be beet red.
Fortunately, it's a beautiful
color and, luckily, it all washes
out easily.*

### Farmer John and Angelic Organics
**Makes 1 Bundt cake**

*Kissing cousin to the old-fashioned red velvet cake (but without the red food dye!), this Chocolate Beet Cake is a rich, moist, sweet cake that is a beautiful dark reddish-brown color. The sweetness of the beets blends beautifully with the honey and maple syrup.—GMB*

**1.** Preheat the oven to 375°F. Lightly coat a 10-cup Bundt pan with oil and dust it with flour.

**2.** Wash the unpeeled beets thoroughly and cut into quarters. Steam them until tender, then grate with a cheese grater. Grate each quarter down to the peel (which provides a nice handle while grating), then discard the peel. You should have about 2 cups of grated beets. Place in a colander and allow the beets to drip while preparing everything else. Using natural sweeteners adds a lot of liquid to the batter, so you don't want it to be too runny. **Note:** *Reducing the amount of liquid in beets is not necessary if you're using the original recipe, which calls for sugar instead of liquid natural sweeteners.*

**3.** Combine the oil, maple syrup, and honey. Stir until well blended. Add the eggs one at a time and beat until fluffy. Add the vanilla extract.

**4.** Sift the flour into a large bowl. Whisk in the cocoa powder, baking soda, and salt. Gently stir the flour mixture into the batter, until it is just mixed. (Do not overmix—the batter will start to rise before you can get it into the oven.)

**5.** Use paper towels and press on top of the grated beets, extracting as much moisture as possible. Fold the beets into the batter, mixing well (but gently), then pour the batter into the pan.

**6.** Bake for about 45 minutes, or until a toothpick inserted into the center comes out clean. Cool for 30 minutes. Carefully invert the pan onto a plate and remove the cake. Serve when cool.

# HONEY STRAWBERRY SHORTCAKES
# WITH HONEY-SWEETENED WHIPPED CREAM

**FRUIT TOPPING**

3 cups local organic strawberries, sliced

⅓ cup mild-flavored local honey, such as orange blossom or wildflower

**SHORTCAKES**

¾ cup unbleached all-purpose flour

¾ cup whole wheat pastry flour

2 teaspoons baking powder

½ teaspoon baking soda

¼ teaspoon salt

6 tablespoons (¾ stick) cold butter, cut into small chunks or grated with a cheese grater

½ cup plus 2 tablespoons chilled buttermilk

3 tablespoons mild-flavored local honey, such as orange blossom or wildflower

**GMB Tip:** *If you happen to have any of the topping left over (chances are you won't!), use it over ice cream or pancakes. Yum.*

**Serves 6**

*Strawberry shortcake is the quintessential spring dessert. Bright red berries, slightly sweetened with your favorite local honey, spill over delicious naturally sweetened shortcake biscuits. The "icing on the cake," of course, is the honey-flavored whipped cream. This same recipe can be used all year long by substituting your favorite in-season fruit. Try blueberries, blackberries, raspberries, or peaches in summer, pears in fall, and apricots in spring. As for winter? This is a fabulous way to use all those berries you froze earlier in the year.—GMB*

**TOPPING**

**1.** Pour the honey over the fruit and mix gently. Let stand 30 to 40 minutes until ready to serve.

**SHORTCAKES**

**1.** Preheat the oven to 400°F.

**2.** Line a baking sheet with parchment paper.

**3.** Combine the dry ingredients in a large mixing bowl. Add the butter. Mix quickly with a fork or pastry blender until the mixture resembles coarse meal.

**4.** Measure the buttermilk in a large measuring cup. Add the honey and stir until mixed.

**5.** Gradually add the buttermilk mixture to the dry ingredients, mixing quickly and gently until there are no dry spots.

**WHIPPED CREAM**

1 cup heavy whipping cream

¼ cup mild-flavored honey, such as orange blossom or wildflower

**6.** Roll out the dough on a floured surface to about ¾-inch thick. Cut out rounds, using a 2½-inch round biscuit cutter.

**7.** Place on prepared baking sheet and bake for about 15 minutes, or until lightly browned.

**8.** Cut each piece of shortcake in half horizontally. Place the bottom half on a plate, top with a spoonful of strawberries, add the other half of the shortcake, and pour more strawberries over it. Finish with a generous dollop of Honey-Sweetened Whipped Cream. Repeat with the other pieces of shortcake and serve warm or at room temperature.

**HONEY-SWEETENED WHIPPED CREAM**

**1.** Making sure the bowl and attachments of an electric mixer are very cold, pour the cream into the bowl and whip until soft peaks begin to form.

**2.** Turn off the mixer and remove the bowl. Carefully pour the honey into the cream and hand whisk it into the cream. Return the bowl to the mixer and finish whipping the cream to desired stiffness. **Note:** *If you pour the honey into the mixing bowl while the mixer is running, the whisk blade will fling strings of honey around the bowl without getting it into the cream. Pretty, but ineffective.*

# APRICOT SQUARES

¾ cup (1½ sticks) softened butter

¾ cup honey

1 egg

½ teaspoon vanilla extract

2 cups whole wheat pastry flour

½ teaspoon baking powder

1⅓ cups shredded coconut

½ cup chopped walnuts

12 ounces (or more) naturally sweetened apricot preserves (1½ cups)

1 apricot, chopped into small pieces

**Makes 36 bars**

*This is a wonderful, moist, sophisticated cookie and a great way to use yummy spring apricots. You can use any kind of jam, of course (as long as it's naturally sweetened). Just match the fresh fruit in the filling with the kind of jam you're using. The small pieces of fresh fruit in the filling makes them particularly delectable.—GMB*

1. Preheat the oven to 350°F.

2. Cream the butter and the honey. Add the egg and mix well. Add the vanilla extract.

3. In a separate bowl, mix the flour and the baking powder.

4. Add the flour mixture to the honey mixture and blend.

5. Fold in the coconut and walnuts.

6. Grease a 13×9×2-inch baking pan.

7. Press about two-thirds of the batter in the bottom of the pan. (Put a piece of plastic wrap over the batter so it won't stick to your fingers as you press it down.) Place the remaining dough in a bowl in the refrigerator while you do the next step.

8. Put the preserves into a bowl and mix in the fresh apricots.

9. Spread this mixture over the batter. Use additional jam if you like more filling.

10. Remove the remaining dough from the refrigerator. Place it between two pieces of floured plastic wrap and roll it until it is approximately the size of the pan. Place this top layer over the filling.

11. Bake 30 to 35 minutes, or until the bars are set and beginning to brown.

12. Cool in the pan, then cut into squares.

# GRAHAM CRACKERS

½ cup all-purpose flour

1¼ cups whole wheat pastry flour

½ cup stone-ground whole wheat flour

1 teaspoon baking powder (non-aluminum)

½ teaspoon baking soda

¼ teaspoon ground cinnamon

½ teaspoon salt

½ cup (1 stick) cold butter, cut into slices

½ cup honey

¼ cup maple syrup

1 teaspoon vanilla extract

**GMB Tips:** *To make these quickly, after you chill the dough put a piece of parchment paper on a baking sheet and roll out the dough directly on the paper. Cut into squares with a pizza cutter, but don't try to separate them; just leave them on the parchment and bake. Take them out of the oven just before they are done. Recut and separate them, allowing the edges to crisp. To cover them with chocolate, melt 4 to 5 ounces of grain-sweetened chocolate chips in the top of a double boiler. Add a tablespoon of either cream or maple syrup to thin it out a little, then spread on top of the graham crackers.*

**Makes 24 squares**

*I love graham crackers, and homemade, naturally sweetened graham crackers are the best. This is an easy, inexpensive recipe. It uses whole wheat pastry flour instead of graham flour. These are fantastic served with honey-sweetened goat cheese and are great slathered with peanut butter and naturally sweetened jelly (see Honey Strawberry Jam recipe on page 68) for a traditional after-school snack. For a more sophisticated treat, cover them with melted grain-sweetened chocolate chips. They're also used as the basis for a homemade graham cracker piecrust.—GMB*

**1.** In a mixing bowl, mix together the flours, baking powder, baking soda, cinnamon, salt, and butter. Mix until the dough resembles coarse meal.

**2.** Mix together the honey, maple syrup, and vanilla extract. Blend in with the dry ingredients and mix until you can form a ball.

**3.** Place the ball between two sheets of parchment paper and gently roll it out to about ½-inch thick. Place in the refrigerator for at least 1 hour to chill.

**4.** Preheat the oven to 350°F.

**5.** Divide the dough into two pieces. Take one piece, put it between two pieces of parchment paper, and roll out to ⅛-inch thick, being careful to roll it evenly.

**6.** Cut the rolled dough into 2-inch squares or cut with cookie cutters. If you want them to look like store-bought graham crackers, prick with a fork. Transfer to a greased cookie sheet (or line with parchment paper).

**7.** Bake for about 15 minutes, or until firm. Serve at room temperature.

# TEETHING BISCUITS

1 cup whole wheat pastry flour

¼ cup spring water

¼ cup barley malt

½ teaspoon orange rind

### Melanie Waxman

**VEGAN**  **LOW-CALORIE**  **EASY**

**Makes 20-24 small cookies**

*This teething biscuit recipe comes from my book* Yummy Yummy in My Tummy—Simply Organic Baby Food Book. *Your baby will enjoy gumming on these healthy teething biscuits.—Melanie*

**1.** Preheat the oven to 300°F.

**2.** Place the flour in a bowl.

**3.** In a separate bowl combine the water, barley malt, and orange rind until it is well mixed.

**4.** Add the barley malt mixture to the flour. Gently mix the ingredients together to form a pliable dough. Add a little more water if it's too dry.

**5.** Roll out the dough and either cut it with a knife or a pizza cutter, or use round cookie cutters to form biscuits that are easy for little fingers to grab. Small, thin rectangular shapes with rounded edges are ideal.

**6.** Bake in the oven for 40 minutes.

**7.** Remove from the oven and allow biscuits to cool for 5 minutes. Store in a container with a lid.

# CARROT HALVA PUDDING

2 teaspoons canola oil

1 small carrot, peeled and shredded (about ½ cup)

Pinch of sea salt

½ teaspoon ground cinnamon

½ teaspoon ground cardamom (optional)

½ teaspoon ground ginger

¾ cup heavy cream

1 large egg, lightly beaten

⅓ cup maple syrup

½ teaspoon vanilla extract

**GMB Tip:** *When preparing the water bath, put the pan—with the ramekins in it—in the oven and then carefully add the water. This way, the water will not spill over into your custard. You generally want to fill water halfway up the sides of your ramekins.*

**Susan Baldassano**

WHEAT-FREE

**Makes six 4-ounce ramekins**

*Halva is a sweet confection popular in the Middle East, Central and Southern Asia, and the Balkans. This pudding is a wonderful and festive way to use spring carrots.—GMB*

**1.** In a small sauté pan, heat oil; add the carrots, salt, cinnamon, cardamom (if using), and ginger.

**2.** Cook on low heat until the carrots soften. Allow them to cool to room temperature.

**3.** Preheat the oven to 325°F.

**4.** In a small bowl whisk the cream, egg, maple syrup, and vanilla extract. Add the carrot mixture and combine.

**5.** Pour the mixture into ramekins. Bake the ramekins in a water bath for about 45 minutes, until the mixture is slightly set, yet still somewhat wobbly.

**6.** Allow the ramekins to cool. Place in the refrigerator for at least 1 hour. Serve chilled.

# SWEET STRAWBERRY PIE

2 pounds fresh strawberries with tops removed, quartered

Juice of half a lemon

1 teaspoon vanilla extract

½ cup brown rice syrup

Pinch of sea salt

2 cups raw almonds

1¾ cups pitted dates

**GMB Tip:** *Room temperature or slightly warm lemons yield the most juice. Microwave the lemon for about 10 seconds (no more), then roll it on the counter with the palm of your hand a few times before you cut it in half.*

*Use a squeezing tool or juicer if you have one. If you don't, just place a strainer over a bowl and hold the lemon over it while simultaneously squeezing it and poking the pulp with a fork.*

## Christina Pirello

**VEGAN**  **WHEAT-FREE**

**Serves 6 to 8**

*Raw cuisine is all the rage, so I decided to play with it. A totally raw approach doesn't work for me, personally, but I think it has definite value to a healthy life. We all need raw foods for enzymes, to aid in digestion, and to create a light, fresh energy. I love to make this pie when strawberries are at the peak of their season of sweet ripeness.*
*—Christina*

**1.** Combine the strawberries, lemon juice, vanilla extract, brown rice syrup, and sea salt in a bowl and toss to combine. Set aside.

**2.** Place the almonds in a blender and pulse on high until they resemble bread crumbs. Empty the almonds onto a plate.

**3.** Place the dates in the blender with about a teaspoon of water and pulse on high until they are well chopped—they will be a little clumpy.

**4.** Combine the almonds and dates until they hold together, then press them evenly onto the bottom and sides of a pie plate to form the crust. Spoon berries generously into the crust, discarding any remaining liquid. Refrigerate for 2 hours before slicing into wedges and serving.

**GMB Tip:** *We found that this worked best when we sliced the strawberries very thin or cut them into small chunks.*

# WHOLE-GRAIN WAFFLES

1 cup whole wheat pastry flour

1 cup mixture of whole-grain flours (such as whole wheat, spelt, cornmeal, rye, or buckwheat)

1½ teaspoons baking powder

1 teaspoon baking soda

½ teaspoon salt

2 cups buttermilk

3 eggs

1 tablespoon sweetener, such as honey or maple syrup (optional)

½ cup (1 stick) butter, melted

**Alice Waters**

**Makes about 8 waffles**

*Sizzling hot from the waffle iron, these whole-grain goodies serve as a wonderful base for fresh farm butter, warm maple syrup, and local spring berries. Although waffles are traditionally eaten at breakfast, these are so good you can eat them for dessert as well—and not feel guilty: They're packed full of whole-grain goodness.—GMB*

**1.** Heat the waffle iron.

**2.** Mix the flours, baking powder, baking soda, and salt together in a large mixing bowl.

**3.** In a large measuring cup, measure the buttermilk, then thoroughly whisk in the eggs and sweetener (if using).

**4.** Pour the buttermilk-and-egg mixture into the dry ingredients and stir until just mixed.

**5.** Add the melted butter and stir until well mixed. If necessary, thin with more buttermilk. The batter should pour off the spoon.

**6.** Cook in the preheated waffle iron until crisp and golden.

**Variations:** *To make waffles with regular milk, increase the baking powder to 2½ teaspoons.*

# HONEY WHOLE WHEAT BREAD

¾ package dry yeast (1¾ teaspoons)

1 cup warm water

6 ounces honey (½ cup)

¾ cup plus 1 tablespoon whole milk

2½ ounces soft butter (5 tablespoons)

2½ cups whole wheat flour

2 teaspoons kosher salt

2 to 3 cups organic bread flour

**Linton Hopkins**

**Makes 2 loaves**

*A real workhorse recipe, this makes a slightly sweet, delicious whole wheat loaf, perfect for toasting in the morning or for making sandwiches. Try it with some homemade pimento cheese or egg salad. It's outstanding.—GMB*

**1.** Dissolve the yeast in warm water. Add two teaspoons of the honey and allow the yeast to sit for 10 minutes, or until foamy.

**2.** Combine the milk, honey, and butter together over low heat until the butter melts. Add this to the yeast.

**3.** In a large bowl, mix the whole wheat flour and salt. Add it to the liquid and stir until well mixed.

**4.** Add one cup of bread flour, then gradually continue to add the remaining flour until the dough forms a ball.

**5.** Knead the dough for 7 to 8 minutes.

**6.** Put the dough in a large, lightly oiled bowl and cover. Place in a warm space until the dough doubles in size.

**7.** Punch down the dough and let rise for 30 minutes.

**8.** Form the dough into loaves and place them in greased loaf pans, or form into rounds and place on a baking sheet. Cover the dough and allow it to rise again until doubled in size.

**9.** Bake for 20 to 25 minutes, or until the bread is baked through and firm to touch.

**Note:** *Baking time is contingent on shape.*

# YOGURT HONEY HEALTH MUFFINS

1½ cups cake flour

1 teaspoon baking powder

1 teaspoon baking soda

¾ teaspoon salt

4½ teaspoons sugar

2 tablespoons rolled oats

1 tablespoon diced dried cranberries

1 tablespoon diced dried apricots

1 tablespoon sunflower seeds, unsalted

1 teaspoon orange zest

1 tablespoon toasted bran

½ cup nonfat yogurt

¼ cup honey

1 teaspoon vanilla extract

½ cup (1 stick) butter, melted

2 eggs

## Chef Ann Cooper

**Makes 24 mini muffins**

*The addition of yogurt makes these muffins moist and nutritionally sound, and they will keep in an airtight container for three days and still taste wonderful. If cake flour is not readily available, all-purpose flour can be substituted. The muffins will be slightly denser, but will taste just as good.—Chef Ann*

**1.** Preheat the oven to 350°F. Prepare a mini muffin pan by either greasing or using liners.

**2.** In a large mixing bowl sift together the flour, baking powder, baking soda, salt, and sugar. Add the oats, dried fruit, sunflower seeds, orange zest, and toasted bran, then mix to combine.

**3.** In a separate bowl, combine yogurt, honey, vanilla extract, butter, and eggs and stir until the ingredients are well blended. Pour the yogurt mixture into the dry ingredients and stir to mix, taking care not to overmix.

**4.** Fill the muffin cups two-thirds full with batter. Bake for approximately 20 minutes, or until golden.

**GMB Tip:** *We also made these with whole wheat pastry flour instead of white flour, and they were exceptionally delicious. They are also good with other dried fruits—dates, raisins, etc.*

# PEANUT BUTTER & JELLY POWER MUFFINS

1 cup whole wheat flour

1½ teaspoons baking powder

1 teaspoon baking soda

½ teaspoon salt

½ cup maple sugar

1 teaspoon ground cinnamon

6 tablespoons rolled oats

3 tablespoons raisins

4 tablespoons raw peanuts

½ cup soy milk

4 tablespoons canola oil

6 tablespoons maple syrup

1 teaspoon vanilla extract

½ cup peanut butter

3 teaspoons cider vinegar

2 medium-sized bananas

4 tablespoons strawberry preserves

## Chef Ann Cooper

**DAIRY-FREE**

**Makes 18 to 20 mini muffins**

*PB & J is a favorite for just about every kid. It's no wonder, then, that this is such a popular muffin with children. A "healthful" muffin, it can be made ahead and stored in the freezer for up to two weeks. To defrost, just remove from the freezer and bring to room temperature, then store in an airtight container for up to three days.—Chef Ann*

**1.** Preheat the oven to 350°F. Prepare a mini muffin pan by either greasing or using liners.

**2.** In a large mixing bowl sift together the flour, baking powder, baking soda, salt, maple sugar, and cinnamon. Add the oats, raisins, and half the peanuts.

**3.** In a separate bowl combine the soy milk, canola oil, maple syrup, vanilla extract, peanut butter, vinegar, and bananas, and mash until all the ingredients are well blended. Pour the peanut butter mix into dry ingredients and stir to mix, taking care not to overmix.

**4.** Fill the muffin cups two-thirds full with batter, then place some preserves (roughly ½ to ¾ teaspoon) onto the top of each muffin. Sprinkle the tops with the remaining peanuts and bake for approximately 20 minutes, or until a toothpick inserted into the center comes out clean.

# TWELVE-GRAIN MUFFINS

½ cup 12-grain cereal (10-grain cereal works, too)

1 cup boiling water

½ cup dates, chopped

1 teaspoon salt

¼ cup honey

2 tablespoons maple syrup

1 egg

¼ cup oil

½ cup buttermilk

1 cup whole wheat flour

2 teaspoons baking powder

1 teaspoon baking soda

1 teaspoon cinnamon

1 cup chopped raw mixed seeds and nuts, such as pumpkin, sesame, flax, sunflower, walnuts, cashews

## Chef Ann Cooper

**Makes 24 mini muffins**

*These muffins were developed by FullBloom Baking Company for the pilot Universal Breakfast program in the Berkeley Unified School District. The muffins are healthful, delicious, and nutritious and are a great component of breakfast. Serve them with your child's favorite flavored yogurt, and breakfast will surely be a hit. They freeze well—in fact, freezing is preferable to refrigeration if you want to save them for more than a couple of days, as it locks moisture in while refrigeration dries food out.—Chef Ann*

**THE NIGHT BEFORE**

**1.** Combine the 12-grain cereal, boiling water, chopped dates, and salt and soak for 8 hours.

**THE NEXT DAY**

**1.** Preheat the oven to 350°F and prepare the mini muffin pan with either cooking spray or paper liners.

**2.** In a small bowl combine the honey, maple syrup, egg, oil, and buttermilk and set aside.

**3.** In a medium bowl combine the flour, baking powder, baking soda, and cinnamon and mix well.

**4.** Mix the cereal mixture from the night before with the mixed wet ingredients, then add it to the mixed dry ingredients, stirring until just combined.

**5.** Bake approximately 20 minutes, or until a toothpick inserted into the center comes out clean.

**GMB Tip:** *If you forget to start these the night before, we found that soaking the cereal and dates for 20 minutes was almost as good.*

# ASPARAGUS-RICOTTA TART
## WITH COMTÉ CHEESE

1 sheet frozen puff pastry (half a 17.3-ounce package)

1 egg, beaten

1 pound slender asparagus spears, trimmed

½ cup whole-milk ricotta cheese

4 teaspoons extra-virgin olive oil, divided

⅛ teaspoon salt

1½ ounces thinly sliced soppressata or other salami, cut into ½-inch pieces

⅔ cup grated Comté cheese (about 3 ounces), divided

Pepper

**Molly Stevens**

**Serves 8 to 10**

*This is one of our favorite recipes, not only because of its taste, but also because it makes a beautiful presentation. You can serve it as a main course or cut it into small squares for a party dish.—GMB*

**1.** Preheat the oven to 400°F.

**2.** Roll out the puff pastry on a lightly floured surface to a 13×10-inch rectangle. Cut off a ½-inch-wide strip from all four sides. Brush strips on one side with some of the beaten egg, then press strips egg-side down onto the edges of pastry to adhere, forming a raised border. Brush border with egg; reserve remaining beaten egg. Transfer to baking sheet. Chill in the refrigerator while preparing the filling.

**3.** Steam asparagus just until crisp-tender, about 3 minutes. Transfer to bowl of ice water to cool. Drain. Cut off the top 2 to 3 inches of asparagus tips; set aside.

**4.** Coarsely puree remaining asparagus stalks in a food processor. Add remaining beaten egg, ricotta, 3 teaspoons oil, and salt; process until a thick puree forms. Transfer the mixture to a bowl; stir in salami and ⅓ cup of the Comté cheese; season with pepper.

**5.** Spread the mixture evenly over the pastry. Sprinkle with the remaining ⅓ cup Comté cheese. Toss the asparagus tips with the remaining 1 teaspoon oil; arrange the tips over the filling.

**6.** Bake the tart until the filling is set, about 25 minutes. Serve warm or at room temperature.

**GMB Tip:** *Comté cheese is a semifirm, Gruyère-style cow's milk cheese. It is available at some supermarkets, cheese shops, and specialty foods stores. You can use Gruyère or Asiago instead, and can substitute prosciutto for the soppressata.*

# VEGETABLE FRITTATA WITH POTATO CRUST

3 medium Yukon gold potatoes

8 large eggs

¾ cup milk

Salt and pepper

4 tablespoons light olive oil, divided

1 medium onion, sliced thin

1 cup cauliflower florets

1 cup broccoli florets

5 tablespoons fresh goat cheese (optional)

## Dan Barber

**WHEAT-FREE**

**Serves 4**

*We are thrilled to include this easy, spring vegetable frittata recipe from Dan. We made it over and over again—it's so good and so easy to make! The potato crust forms a perfect base for the eggs and vegetables. Enjoy!—GMB*

**1.** Preheat the oven to 375°F.

**2.** Boil the potatoes in a medium-sized pot of well-salted water. When the potatoes are tender, drain and cool.

**3.** Beat the eggs with the milk and season with salt and pepper to taste.

**4.** In a 10-inch nonstick sauté pan, heat 3 tablespoons of the olive oil over medium heat. Add the onions, cauliflower, and broccoli and sauté for about 8 minutes. Remove the vegetables from the pan.

**5.** Cool the pan slightly and add 1 additional tablespoon of olive oil. Gently press the cooked potatoes into an even layer in the pan. Top with the sautéed vegetables. Pour egg mixture over the vegetables and spoon small chunks of goat cheese on top.

**6.** Bake for about 20 minutes, or until the top is golden brown and the eggs have just set.

**7.** Remove from the oven and slide frittata out of the pan and onto a cutting board. Cut into wedges and serve warm.

# ASPARAGUS FLAN
## WITH SMOKED SALMON POTATO SALAD

1 pound asparagus, tips trimmed to about 4 inches, the rest chopped (except woody ends)

1 teaspoon butter

2 tablespoons shallots, chopped

2 cups whipping cream, plus a little more, as needed

3 egg yolks plus 1 whole egg

Salt and pepper

Nutmeg

**Susan Spicer**

**Makes six 4-ounce servings**

*Try this for a wonderful light spring dinner or a scrumptious brunch. The combination of the asparagus with the smoked salmon is outstanding.*—GMB

**1.** Preheat the oven to 325°F.

**2.** Blanch the asparagus tips in boiling water for about 2 to 3 minutes, then shock them in ice water and set aside.

**3.** Melt the butter in a small pot and add the shallots. Cook for 2 minutes, then add the chopped asparagus ends and the whipping cream. Simmer gently for about 10 minutes or until asparagus pieces are tender. Remove from the heat and let cool for about 5 minutes, then pour into a blender and puree until smooth. Strain and reserve liquid.

**4.** Measure and add more cream (if needed) to make 2 to 2¼ cups asparagus cream.

**5.** In a bowl, whisk the egg yolks and whole egg together until well mixed and just barely frothy. Gently whisk in asparagus cream and season with salt, pepper, and nutmeg to taste.

**6.** Pour the mixture into buttered ramekins or custard dishes, cover with foil, and bake in a water bath for about 30 minutes. Open the foil and jiggle the pan to see if the flans are set. They should be firm around the outside but just barely set in the middle, with no bubbles. If they are still liquid in the middle, return them to the oven and check again after 10 minutes. When ready, remove them from the oven, uncover, and set aside until ready to serve.

# SMOKED SALMON POTATO SALAD

2 tablespoons finely chopped shallots

3 tablespoons malt, sherry, or white wine vinegar

6 tablespoons olive oil

1 cup baking potatoes, diced and boiled until tender but not mushy

3 tablespoons finely chopped celery

3 tablespoons chopped red onion

½ cup toasted bread croutons

½ cup smoked salmon

2 tablespoons crisp bacon

Salt and pepper

**1.** Whisk the shallots, vinegar, and olive oil together in a small bowl. In a separate bowl, mix the potatoes, celery, red onions, croutons, and salmon.

**2.** Stir in half the dressing, season with salt and pepper, toss, and add more dressing to desired taste. Add the bacon and toss again, then divide salad between plates and place one warm flan on each plate.

# FENNEL AND MUSHROOM PIE

1 pound new potatoes, scrubbed and sliced

2 tablespoons whole milk

1 tablespoon butter

1 fennel bulb, roughly cut

1 large carrot, sliced

2 tablespoons light olive oil

2 onions, finely chopped

1 clove garlic, minced

½ pound mushrooms, sliced

Salt and pepper

¼ cup bread crumbs

2 tablespoons chopped fresh parsley

¼ cup fresh basil

8 ounces mozzarella cheese, grated

8 ounces cheddar cheese, grated

**Serves 6 to 8**

*The incomparable taste of fennel makes this a wonderful and unique dish. The fennel complements the potatoes and mushrooms beautifully, offering a healthful, seasonal dish great for a vegetarian dinner.—GMB*

**1.** Preheat the oven to 400°F.

**2.** Cook the potatoes in salted boiling water for 10 to 15 minutes, until tender. Drain, then mash with a potato masher. While potatoes are still hot, mix in the milk and butter.

**3.** Cook the roughly chopped fennel and the sliced carrot in salted boiling water for about 7 minutes, until tender, then drain.

**4.** Heat olive oil in a sauté pan, add onions, and cook for 5 to 10 minutes, until they begin to brown. Add the garlic and cook for another minute. Add the mushrooms and cook for another 2 minutes. Season with salt and pepper.

**5.** Sprinkle half the bread crumbs over the base of a shallow, ovenproof 9-inch baking dish. Add half the mushrooms and onions, fennel, parsley, basil, mozzarella and cheddar cheeses, and potatoes in layers. Repeat the layer, finishing with potatoes. Bake for 20 to 30 minutes, or until heated through.

**GMB Tip:** *To make this wheat-free, just substitute ¼ cup of rolled oats or ⅓ cup of finely chopped almonds for the bread crumbs. To make it dairy-free, use vegan cheese, soy milk, and a butter substitute.*

# SPINACH AND GOAT CHEESE TURNOVERS

1 tablespoon light olive oil

½ green onion, chopped

2 cloves of garlic, minced

2 large bunches of fresh spinach, stemmed and chopped

2 ounces soft fresh goat cheese

⅓ cup toasted pine nuts

3 tablespoons grated parmesan cheese

½ teaspoon chopped herbs, such as rosemary, parsley, or chives

1 teaspoon lemon zest

Salt and pepper

4 frozen phyllo pastry sheets, thawed

½ cup (1 stick) unsalted butter, melted

**Makes 12**

*This calls for store-bought phyllo dough, making it an easy recipe. It's an excellent way to use fresh spring spinach. For variety, mix and match the greens and include chopped arugula or chard. This is great paired with a simple salad of spring greens and strawberries. Finish off this light, fresh meal with a cup of tea and Apricot Squares (page 50) for dessert.—GMB*

**1.** Heat the olive oil in a large heavy skillet over medium heat. Add the onion and garlic and sauté for 5 minutes. Increase the heat to high. Add the spinach and sauté until it has wilted, about 5 minutes. Drain spinach mixture, pressing on solids to release as much liquid as possible.

**2.** Transfer spinach mixture to a bowl and cool completely. Add the goat cheese, pine nuts, parmesan, herbs, and lemon zest. Season to taste with salt and pepper.

**3.** Place one phyllo sheet on a work surface. Cut the phyllo lengthwise equally into 3 strips. Brush one of the dough strips with butter. Place 1 rounded tablespoon of filling at one end of the dough strip. Starting at a corner, fold the pastry over the filling, forming a triangle.

**4.** Repeat, folding up the length of the pastry, keeping the triangle shape. Brush with more butter. Repeat with the remaining pastry, butter, and filling.

**5.** Transfer the turnovers to a baking sheet. Cover and chill for at least 30 minutes.

**6.** Preheat the oven to 375°F while they chill.

**7.** Bake about 12 minutes, or until the turnovers are golden. Cool slightly and serve.

# APRICOTS WITH ROSE PETAL-BLOSSOM HONEY SYRUP

8 slightly ripe but firm apricots, washed

Squeeze of fresh lemon juice

Rose Petal–Blossom Honey Syrup (see recipe on opposite page)

½ cup crème fraîche (sour cream can be substituted)

## Carrie Nahabedian

**WHEAT-FREE**

**Serves 4**

*This dessert compote can be made with fresh or dried apricots. If using dried apricots, they need to be soaked in water for an hour before poaching in the syrup. I like this dish served chilled, but it can also be served warm. Very intense and floral, the rose petals get "preserved" in the syrup.—Carrie*

**1.** Make a slit in the bottom of each apricot and blanch them in boiling water with the lemon juice for approximately 20 seconds, just until the apricot skin relaxes. With a slotted spoon, remove from water and place quickly in an ice bath. Slip the pit out.

**2.** Make the Rose Petal-Blossom Honey Syrup.

**3.** Using a medium-sized pot, carefully put the apricots into the warm syrup. Cook slowly over low heat for 5 minutes, then remove from heat. Place a plate over the top of the pot and let the apricots sit in the syrup to absorb the aroma and flavors of the syrup.

**4.** After 15 minutes, remove the apricots, let them cool, and refrigerate until they are chilled. Fill the pit indentation with a touch (approximately ¼ teaspoon) of crème fraîche (or sour cream).

**5.** Put the apricots in a serving bowl with approximately 1 teaspoon of crème fraîche. Drizzle apricots with the syrup and serve.

# ROSE PETAL–BLOSSOM HONEY SYRUP

1½ cup mild flavored honey, such as clover or wildflower

½ cup water

¼ cup fresh-squeezed lemon juice

Zest of 1 lemon

1 cup bright red fragrant rose petals, cleaned and dried with white flesh removed

1 tablespoon rose water (optional)

**Makes about 2 cups**

**1.** Put all the ingredients into a heavy saucepot and bring to a boil over medium-high heat, then reduce to a simmer. Stir so the flavor of the rose petals perfumes the syrup. Continue cooking and reduce by half, or until the honey syrup has reached a viscous consistency (but not too thick—just enough to lightly coat the back of a spoon).

**2.** If you desire a very intense floral fragrance, add the rose water.

**3.** Chill.

**Note:** *This syrup can be stored in a refrigerator for 1 week.*

# HONEY STRAWBERRY JAM

6 cups chopped strawberries

1½ boxes pectin

1½ cups honey

2 tablespoons fresh lemon juice

**Makes 6 cups**

*This is a great way to make the best use of a lot of berries during the peak season. The honey lends a unique flavor to the jam. Put the jam into small jars and you'll have your Christmas gifts done in June! The jam can also be used in many different recipes, including Evan Pierce's Thumbprint Cookies (page 87) or in Chef Ann Cooper's Peanut Butter & Jelly Power Muffins (page 58).—GMB*

**1.** Wash and sterilize six small jelly jars.

**2.** Mash the berries. Add the pectin, place in a large saucepan, and bring to a rolling boil.

**3.** Stir and boil for 1 minute. Remove from the heat and add the honey and lemon juice. Bring to a boil again and continue to boil for 5 minutes, stirring continually.

**4.** Using oven mitts, ladle mixture into hot jars. Put lids on jars and immerse in hot water bath for 8 minutes. Place on a counter and allow to cool thoroughly.

**Note:** *For more information about canning and preserving, see "Preserving the Harvest," pages 185–190.*

# RHUBARB COMPOTE

6 cups fresh rhubarb, trimmed and chopped

2 tart crisp apples, such as Granny Smith, peeled, cored, and cubed

½ cup fresh orange juice

½ cup maple sugar

2 cinnamon sticks

1 to 2 cups fresh strawberries, hulled and halved

**Chef Bev Shaffer**

**Makes about 9 cups**

*For a wonderful spring dessert, try this: Slice angel food cake into serving-size pieces. Place them on parchment paper-lined cookie sheets, and toast in a 325°F oven until slices are crisp and lightly golden on top. Top with the rhubarb compote for something special.
—Chef Bev*

**1.** Combine all the ingredients except the strawberries in a medium saucepan. Bring to boil over medium heat, then cover and simmer for 5 minutes, or until rhubarb begins to soften.

**2.** Uncover and continue to cook for additional 3 to 4 minutes.

**3.** Taking the saucepan off the heat, remove the cinnamon sticks. Add the strawberries, stirring gently to combine. Serve.

Basil
Blackberries
Blueberries
Cherries
Corn
Figs
Garlic
Huckleberries
Lemon balm
Melons
Mint
Nectarines
Peaches
Peppers (sweet bell)
Plums
Raspberries
Tomatoes
Yellow squash
Zucchini

# SUMMER

For several years I spent my summers in Swan Valley, Montana. People go to Montana for different reasons, most often for the fly-fishing or hiking, or simply to enjoy the incredible beauty. I went to Montana for the huckleberries. Late July and early August is huckleberry season, and every year I waded into thickets rich with the unique aroma of these small bluish purple berries. I happily risked attack from everything from mosquitoes to grizzly bears to pick the berries, each one about the size of an English pea. Hours of picking yielded only a couple of small baskets of these delicious berries, but I counted those hours as well spent. If you're a berry-picking nut like me, you'll understand. Nothing can keep a wild berry–picking fanatic from his or her berries—the fruit of the vine is just too sweet.

Of course, picking the berries was just the beginning. Every year I'd enter the Swan Valley Huckleberry Baking Contest, and every year I'd lose to the locals who came up with the most innovative and fantastic ways to use these wild berries, from jams and jellies to fruit leathers and jerkies, to pies, cobblers, cakes, cookies, and more.

Fortunately, you don't have to risk attack from grizzly bears to be able to enjoy the fabulous fruits and vegetables of summer. They're available, in abundance, in almost every community, and if you can't pick or grow your own, you can probably find them at a local farmers' market.

Summer farmers' markets are brilliantly colorful. From fiery red tomatoes to green peppers, yellow squash to purple plums, the colors of summer will fill your plate and your palate. Our contributors have come up with some fabulous recipes to use these fresh and wonderful fruits and vegetables. One of our favorite recipes is Rozanne Gold's Yellow Squash and Sun-dried Tomato "Quiche" (page 105). Not only is it one of the best things we've eaten, it's also one of the quickest to make—which is always a plus during the busy days of summer. If you have an abundance of stone fruits, try slicing them into Elizabeth Crane's Peach and Nectarine Upside-down Cake (pages 82–83). You might even want to try my very own Huckleberry (or blueberry) Sour Cream Pie (page 91), even though I did lose the baking contest to the sheriff's daughter!

• • • • • • •

## Choosing Produce

**BLUEBERRIES** The blueberry is indigenous to North America. Native Americans dried them in the sun and used them in soups and stews. They also crushed the dried berries and rubbed them on meat as a preservative. Look for plump, smooth berries with no wrinkles. Blueberries are easy to freeze— just put them on a cookie sheet in the freezer for an hour or so, then pack them in a freezer container and mark with the date. These will last about a year. Frozen blueberries are great to use in scones, cakes, cookies, and such. Don't thaw them out first, just add them frozen directly to the recipe.

**The U. S. Highbush Blueberry Council tips for baking with blueberries:**

-When you add blueberries to batter, do so at the end of the process and do not overmix. If you're using frozen blueberries, do not thaw them out before adding them to the batter.

- To keep blueberries from sinking down to the bottom of the batter, mix a little flour or cornstarch into the blueberries before adding them to the batter, or spread half the batter in the pan, add the blueberries, and pour the rest of the batter on top. When making blueberry pancakes, pour the batter onto the skillet first, then add the berries.

**CHERRIES** The best cherries are firm, without blemishes, and still have their stems. Cherries that have already lost their stems have a break in the skin that makes them more susceptible to decay. Take time to look through and choose the best fruit. Place unwashed cherries in a plastic container and put them in the refrigerator. They should last five to six days, but be sure to check for and remove any decayed or soft fruit. Cherries freeze well: Place washed cherries in a single layer on a cookie sheet in the freezer. Once frozen, place the cherries in a freezer container and mark with the date. Frozen cherries should be good for up to a year.

CORN Buy corn that has bright, closely spaced kernels. Buy it in the husk, if possible, and pull down the husk a little to see what each piece looks like. If it's wrinkled or dried out, don't buy it (though it's normal for the very tip to look a little less than perfect). Ideally, corn should go straight from the garden to the cooking pot to the plate, but it will be fine if kept in the refrigerator for a few days.

When buying cornmeal, look for the stone-ground variety. Buy it from a local miller, if possible.

GARLIC Choose garlic bulbs that have tightly packed cloves with smooth skins and no green coming out of the top. Don't put these in the refrigerator, but keep them in a cool, dry place. They should last for a couple of weeks.

NECTARINES Many people consider nectarines a smaller and sweeter version of a peach. Nectarines will continue to ripen after they have been picked, meaning you can safely choose nectarines that have not completely ripened yet. They should have a nice yellowish red color, though, and be slightly firm to the touch. Don't buy nectarines that are green or hard. They taste best when eaten at room temperature. Because nectarines do not have the same fuzz on their skin as peaches do, it's not necessary to peel them. Allow nectarines to ripen at room temperature. Store in the refrigerator when fully ripened. They should last a couple of weeks.

PEACHES Peaches should be picked when ripe, not before. Although a peach will get softer and juicier after it is picked, it will not get any sweeter. Choose fruit that shows the "blush" characteristic of the fruit. Different kinds of peaches are different shades of yellow, orange, and red, so color alone is not a good indicator of ripeness. As soon as the peach emits a sweet, peachy smell, refrigerate until you're ready to use. To peel peaches easily, put them in boiling water for about 15 seconds, then immediately submerse in ice water. Slice peaches and put in a freezer container, marked with the date. Peaches freeze well.

Peaches retain more toxins from sprays and chemicals than any other fruit. If possible, always choose organic peaches.

**PEPPERS (SWEET BELL)** Summer bell peppers include the green, orange, red, and yellow varieties. Choose peppers that are firm and glossy without any soft spots, puckering, or withering. They keep well in the refrigerator for several days and can be frozen (without blanching) for later use. Freeze as you would blueberries (see above).

**PLUMS** Choose fruit that is slightly soft but that does not show any signs of decay (shriveled skin or dark, soft spots). Like peaches, plums do not get sweeter as they ripen. And, like peaches, the skins slip off easily when treated with the boiling water and ice water routine, explained under the entry about peaches. Store ripe plums in the refrigerator for up to two weeks.

**TOMATOES** Ideally, you'll find firm, plump, heavy fruit without dark or soft spots, but in actuality, tomatoes from small farms are full of character. Choose the freshest-looking ones possible and just work around any blemishes. Be sure the tomatoes are not overripe, as they will be soft and mushy. Tomatoes are best when eaten right off the vine, but they can be stored at room temperature for a few days. If you know you cannot use them within a day or two, store in the refrigerator. This decreases the flavor but allows for a longer shelf life. Before using, wash and remove the stem, if necessary. Peeled, chopped tomatoes can be frozen and used in soups, stews, and sauces. Place in a freezer container, marked with the date.

**YELLOW SUMMER SQUASH AND ZUCCHINI** Choose small, tender squash (less than eight inches) with thin skins. Store in a plastic container in the refrigerator up to five days. When ready to use, wash and cut both stem ends and slice as needed. You can freeze grated zucchini, measured in amounts you'll need in recipes.

# ALL-ORGANIC SPECIAL OCCASION CAKE

2 cups minus 1 tablespoon organic unbleached white flour

1 tablespoon arrowroot

1 teaspoon salt

4 teaspoons baking powder

2 cups organic whole wheat pastry flour (or additional unbleached white flour)

1½ cups (3 sticks) organic butter, at room temperature

1½ cups agave nectar

½ cup milk

8 organic eggs

2 teaspoons organic vanilla extract (or other flavoring, such as almond)

**GMB Tip:** *If you are making a cake with different size tiers, find out how many cups of batter you need for each pan size and make the number of recipes needed. It's best to make each batch separately rather than measuring and mixing multiple batches of this recipe all at once. If you are making this cake for a large event, you should make a small test cake first.*

**Debra Lynn Dadd**

Makes 8 cups of batter, which will fill one of the following: (1) one 12×17×1-inch half sheet (make two batches of the recipe if you want a two-layer cake this size), (2) two 8-inch rounds, or (3) one 9×13-inch rectangle

**1.** Preheat the oven to 325°F. Butter and flour the cake pan, then line it with parchment paper.

**2.** Measure 2 cups of white flour, then remove one tablespoon of flour and replace it with 1 tablespoon of arrowroot. **Note:** *This is essential to the recipe! Do not leave it out!*

**3.** Add the salt and baking powder, then sift together with the whole wheat pastry flour. (Some whole wheat chaff will be left in sifter—put it back in the bowl with the flours.)

**4.** Using an electric mixer, cream the butter until fluffy. Add the sweetener gradually, beating until light and fluffy.

**5.** Add the eggs to the butter, one at a time, beating well after each addition.

**6.** Measure the milk in a liquid measuring cup and add the vanilla extract.

**7.** Sift the flour mixture into the butter mixture, alternating with the milk and vanilla extract. Stir until well blended.

**8.** Pour the batter into the prepared pan and bake. A half-sheet pan takes about 50 minutes to bake. Smaller sizes take less time, probably about 30 minutes. The cake is done when a toothpick inserted in the center comes out clean.

**9.** Let the cake cool in the pan for about 10 minutes, then remove it from the pan and let it cool completely on a wire rack.

# BLUEBERRY GRUNT

FILLING

- 4 cups fresh or frozen blueberries
- ¼ cup date sugar (or maple sugar)
- ½ cup honey
- ¼ cup water
- 3 tablespoons fresh lemon juice
- 2 teaspoons lemon zest
- ¼ teaspoon nutmeg

DUMPLINGS

- 1½ cups whole wheat pastry flour
- 1½ tablespoons date sugar (or maple sugar)
- 2 teaspoons baking powder
- ¾ teaspoon sea salt
- 3 tablespoons unsalted butter, chilled
- ¾ cup whole milk

## CulinaryCorps

**Serves 8 to 10**

*This Blueberry Grunt recipe comes from an event in Ocean Springs, Mississippi, where the CulinaryCorps group actually picked the blueberries at a farm in the morning and used them that night at a Slow Food Gala where local goods were the spotlight. Fresh berries make this dessert really special, but frozen ones will do just fine.*
*—CulinaryCorps*

**1.** To make the filling, place all the filling ingredients in a 12-inch skillet. Bring it to a boil over medium heat, then reduce heat to low and cook about 10 to 15 minutes, or until the berries are soft and the juice is slightly thicker.

**2.** Meanwhile, prepare the dumplings by whisking together the dry ingredients. Using a pastry blender or fork, blend the cold butter into the mixture until it resembles bread crumbs. Add the milk until it is incorporated and a sticky dough has formed.

**3.** Drop tablespoons of dough into the simmering blueberries, placing the dumplings so they touch one another. Cover the skillet and cook on medium-low for about 25 minutes, or until dumplings are firm and a toothpick inserted into the dumplings comes out clean. Serve warm with naturally sweetened vanilla ice cream or freshly whipped cream.

# NEW YORK-STYLE CHEESECAKE

**FILLING**

4 8-ounce packages cream cheese, at room temperature (use natural cream cheese if you can find it)

¾ cup agave nectar

¼ cup flour

5 eggs

1 teaspoon Mexican vanilla extract

**CRUST**

2 cups graham cracker crumbs, store-bought or homemade (see Graham Crackers on page 51)

½ cup (1 stick) butter, melted

**GMB Tip:** *Serve this naturally sweetened cheesecake with your favorite fruit of the moment and you'll have a sensational seasonal dessert. It takes a while to bake and cool this cake, so start early in the day. This is classy, beautiful, and absolutely delicious.*

**Volcanic Nectar Company**

Serves 12 to 16

**FILLING**

**1.** Preheat the oven to 350°F. To make the filling, combine the cream cheese, agave nectar, and flour in the bowl of an electric mixer. Beat until smooth. Add the eggs one at a time, beating well after each addition. Add the vanilla extract.

**2.** Pour the cream cheese mixture over the crust and bake for 15 minutes. Lower the oven temperature to 200°F and bake for an additional 1 hour and 30 minutes, or until the center no longer looks wet and shiny.

**3.** Turn the oven off. Let the cheesecake cool in the oven for 1 hour with the door ajar. Remove from the oven and place the springform pan on a rack to cool completely.
**Tip:** *To prevent the top of the cheesecake from cracking, run a knife around the edge of the pan so that the cake can pull away freely as it contracts.*

**4.** Cover and refrigerate the cheesecake for at least 4 hours before removing it from the springform pan and serving.

**GRAHAM CRACKER CRUST**

**1.** To make the crust, in a small bowl stir together the graham cracker crumbs and butter until well blended. (Add a little agave nectar if it won't cling together well.) Press the mixture evenly onto the bottom and sides of a greased 9-inch springform pan; set aside. **Note:** *If you cover the crumb mixture with plastic wrap, you can use your fingers to press it down without the crumbs sticking to your fingers.*

# ENGLISH FRUIT TRIFLE

½ recipe All-Organic Special Occasion Cake (see recipe, page 76)

1 recipe vanilla custard (see Blackberry Tart, page 89)

1 cup Honey Strawberry Jam (store-bought or see recipe on page 68)

Zest of 1 lemon

1 cup dry sherry

3 tablespoons brandy

2 to 3 cups fresh seasonal fruits, peeled and cut

2 cups whipping cream, sweetened with 1 tablespoon maple syrup

**Serves 8 to 10**

*This is a beautiful, elegant way to take advantage of the fruits of summer. You can use whatever is available, such as blueberries, blackberries, peaches, or strawberries—anything you have in abundance. You can even use bananas by themselves for a naturally sweetened version of that old favorite, banana pudding. To make it "family friendly," use peach nectar instead of the sherry and brandy, but for a sophisticated adult dessert, the liqueurs add a special touch. Be sure you allow the trifle to chill in the refrigerator for several hours, or overnight, so the cake can soak up all the wonderful flavors.—GMB*

**1.** Early in the day, make the cake, baking it in a 9×13-inch pan. Allow it to cool thoroughly.

**2.** Make the custard and allow it to cool in the refrigerator for several hours.

**3.** Cut half the cake into long slivers, about 1 inch wide. Break each of these long slivers into pieces about 2½ inches long, then cut through these lengthwise. You should end up with pieces of cake about the size of a ladyfinger.

**4.** Cover the bottom of a trifle bowl with the ladyfinger cake pieces, then cover with half the strawberry jam. Pour half the sherry and half the brandy over this, then sprinkle with half the lemon zest. Cover with half the sliced fruit and allow it to stand for about an hour.

**5.** Pour half the custard over the fruit and repeat the layers of cake, jam, sherry, brandy, lemon zest, and fruit. Pour the remaining custard over the top layer and chill for several hours. Just before serving, cover with sweetened whipped cream and almond slivers or slices of fruit and berries.

# BOBOTA (GREEK CORNBREAD) WITH HONEY ORANGE SYRUP

1 cup plus 2 tablespoons all-purpose flour

1 cup plus 2 tablespoons stone-ground cornmeal

2 teaspoons baking powder

½ teaspoon baking soda

¼ teaspoon salt

4 eggs, separated

½ cup (1 stick) butter, at room temperature

½ cup honey*

Zest of 1 orange

¾ cup freshly squeezed orange juice**

1 cup currants or raisins

Honey Orange Syrup (recipe on opposite page)

\* *original recipe called for ½ cup sugar*

\*\* *original recipe called for 1 cup orange juice*

**Crescent Dragonwagon**

Serves 9 to 12

*We have adapted Crescent's wonderful recipe (with her permission) to make it with natural sweeteners (we used honey since there was already honey in the syrup). This makes an incredibly moist, sweet cake rich with orange flavor. The cornmeal adds an interesting texture that beautifully complements the plump currants. Even without the Honey Orange Syrup, this is a fabulous dish.—GMB*

**1.** Preheat the oven to 350°F. Oil a 9-inch square pan and set it aside.

**2.** In a medium bowl, sift together the flour, cornmeal, baking powder, baking soda, and salt. Set aside.

**3.** In a clean, dry mixing bowl, whip the egg whites until stiff. Set aside.

**4.** In a separate bowl, cream together the butter and honey. Add the egg yolks one at a time, then add the orange zest. Add the flour mixture and the orange juice, stirring until combined. Fold in the egg whites and currants or raisins.

**5.** Spoon the batter into the prepared pan and bake 35 to 40 minutes, or until firm, golden brown, and slightly domed in middle. As the cake bakes, prepare the Honey Orange Syrup.

**6.** When the cake is done, remove it from the oven and prick it all over with a toothpick. Pour the Honey Orange Syrup evenly over the cake. Let it stand 1 to 2 hours before serving.

# HONEY ORANGE SYRUP

½ cup honey*

　Juice from one orange, plus enough water to make 1 cup total liquid

6 whole cloves

* *original recipe called for ½ cup sugar plus 3 tablespoons honey*

**1.** In a small saucepan over medium-high heat, combine all the ingredients.

**2.** Bring to a boil, then reduce to a simmer, and cook about 4 minutes, or until the mixture becomes a thin syrup.

**3.** Let it cool to room temperature. Remove the cloves before pouring over the cornbread.

# PEACH AND NECTARINE UPSIDE-DOWN CAKE

## TOPPING

1½ pounds firm, just-ripe yellow peaches and nectarines (about 3 to 4 pieces of fruit)

½ cup (1 stick) unsalted butter

½ cup maple syrup*

\* original recipe called for ½ cup sugar instead of maple syrup

### Elizabeth Crane

**Makes one 10-inch round cake**

*In other seasons, this cake is great with apples or pears instead of peaches and nectarines. You could use grated apple in the batter, too. You can even make this cake with canned pineapple slices. Try different flavorings in the cake, like orange zest instead of ginger, and/or flavored yogurt instead of sour cream. The topping takes 30 minutes to cook, so be sure to start the topping first, before you make the cake batter.—Elizabeth*

### TOPPING

**1.** Peel and quarter the fruit. In an ovenproof 10-inch skillet over low heat, melt the butter and stir in the maple syrup. Place the peach and nectarine quarters flat-side down in the butter syrup, and let the mixture cook over very low heat until it darkens and the fruit is soft, about 30 minutes.

**2.** While the topping cooks, prepare the cake.

CAKE

1½ cups all-purpose flour

1½ teaspoons baking powder

¾ teaspoon salt

½ cup (1 stick) unsalted butter, softened

¼ cup brown rice syrup* (or honey)

¼ cup maple syrup*

1 teaspoon vanilla extract

1 teaspoon grated fresh ginger

2 eggs

½ cup sour cream (or plain yogurt)

½ peach (with its juice), peeled and chopped

*\* original recipe called for ½ cup sugar instead of syrups*

**GMB Tip:** *For a little extra kick, add chopped candied ginger to the cake batter and add coarsely chopped nuts (walnuts, almonds) to the topping as it cooks. When baking, this cake may overflow. You might want to put a pan or a piece of aluminum foil underneath to catch the drips.*

CAKE

**1.** Preheat the oven to 375°F.

**2.** Stir together the flour, baking powder, and salt. Set aside.

**3.** In a separate bowl, beat together the butter, syrups (and/or honey), vanilla extract, and ginger.

**4.** Add the eggs one at a time. Stir in the sour cream (or yogurt).

**5.** Gradually add the flour mixture to the egg mixture until just combined. Add the peach (with juice).

**6.** When the topping is ready and the cake batter is mixed, take the skillet off the heat and spoon the batter over the fruit, leaving a half-inch border uncovered around the edges (the cake will expand to cover all the fruit).

**7.** Bake for about 30 minutes, or until a toothpick inserted into the cake's center comes out clean.

**8.** Cool the cake in the pan for 10 minutes, then run a knife around the rim to loosen and carefully invert it onto a plate. Serve warm with vanilla ice cream.

# PLUM AND WALNUT UPSIDE-DOWN CAKE

## TOPPING

5 tablespoons unsalted butter, divided, at room temperature

⅛ cup maple syrup

¼ cup local wildflower honey

½ cup chopped walnuts, toasted

10 Castleton plums (or any small local plum), halved and pitted

**Christine Carroll**

**Serves 8**

*A twist on the 1950s pineapple classic, this upside-down cake features local plums as excellent understudies. Their sweet-tart profile affords plums versatility, allowing this cake to be on your brunch sideboard or part of your dessert repertoire.—Christine*

### TOPPING

**1.** Lightly butter an 8-inch round cake pan with 1 tablespoon of butter, concentrating on the sides of the pan, and set it aside.

**2.** In a small saucepan over medium-high heat, combine the remaining butter, maple syrup, and honey. Heat about 1 minute, or until combined. Reduce heat to medium and continue to cook about 5 minutes, or until thick.

**3.** Pour the maple syrup mixture into the cake pan, turning it to coat the bottom evenly. Sprinkle the walnuts evenly onto the syrup mixture.

**4.** Cut each plum half into thirds (approximately ¾ inch wide) and arrange the fruit in the bottom of the cake pan in overlapping concentric circles.

CAKE

- ¾ cup whole wheat flour
- ¾ cup unbleached white flour
- 2 teaspoons baking powder
- ½ teaspoon ground cinnamon
- ¼ teaspoon ground sea salt
- 1 teaspoon arrowroot
- 6 tablespoons unsalted butter, at room temperature
- ½ cup local wildflower honey
- ⅛ cup maple syrup
- 1 teaspoon vanilla extract
- 2 jumbo local eggs
- ¼ cup buttermilk

CAKE

**1.** Preheat the oven to 350°F.

**2.** In a bowl, combine the flours, baking powder, cinnamon, salt, and arrowroot. Set aside.

**3.** In a standing mixer with the paddle attachment, whip the butter for about 1 minute, until it is light and airy. Add the honey, vanilla extract, and maple syrup, beating for 2 more minutes, scraping the sides as necessary to incorporate.

**4.** Reduce the speed to low and add the eggs, one at a time, until well mixed, then alternate adding the dry ingredients and buttermilk to the bowl. Mix until just blended.

**5.** Spread the batter evenly over the plums (the cake pan will be filled almost to the top). Bake on the middle rack of the oven for 65 minutes, or until a toothpick inserted in the center comes out clean.

**6.** Run a small knife around the inside edge of the pan to loosen the sides of the cake. Place a plate on top of the cake pan. Gently invert the pan onto the plate and tap the bottom of the cake pan lightly to help release the cake from the pan. Gently lift the cake pan off the cake. Allow the cake to cool for 5 minutes. Serve warm with whipped cream.

**GMB Tip:** *This cake has more cake than topping. If you prefer a more equal ratio, remove 1 cup of the cake batter after mixing and discard (or bake in a small loaf pan), then proceed with the recipe as written.*

# ALMOND COOKIES

1 cup finely ground brown rice flour

½ teaspoon baking powder

¼ cup (½ stick) butter, softened

¼ cup honey or agave nectar

1 egg

1 teaspoon almond extract

1 to 2 teaspoons water
Blanched whole almonds

**Marlene Bumgarner**

**WHEAT-FREE**

**Makes 1 dozen**

*This is a perfect little cookie for anyone, but is especially appreciated by those with a gluten intolerance, or for the growing number of people who are simply trying to eat less wheat. It's great for serving with a bowl of Maple Ice Cream (see page 149) or Chocolate Tofu Pudding (see page 170).—GMB*

**1.** Preheat the oven to 350°F.

**2.** In a small bowl, stir together the rice flour and baking powder, pressing out any lumps.

**3.** In a separate bowl, blend the butter, honey or agave nectar, egg, and almond extract. Add the flour mixture, adding enough water to form the dough into balls.

**4.** Roll the dough into balls about the size of a walnut and place them on a lightly greased baking sheet. Flatten the balls slightly with the floured bottom of a glass (or roll the dough out to ½-inch thickness and cut with a round cookie cutter).

**5.** Press a whole almond into the center of each cookie. Brush them with milk or egg yolk for glazed, brown effect.

**6.** Bake for 20 minutes or until slightly brown around the edges.

# THUMBPRINT COOKIES

1 cup (2 sticks) unsalted butter, at room temperature

⅓ cup honey

1 tablespoon vanilla extract

1 teaspoon salt

1 cup pecan meal

2 cups whole wheat pastry flour

**Evan Price, Blue Heron Bakery**

**Makes 2 to 2½ dozen cookies**

*This is one of the Blue Heron Bakery's most popular cookies. It's a versatile recipe that can be changed to use different fillings, depending on what you have available. It's also pretty and fancy enough to serve at a party.—GMB*

**1.** Preheat the oven to 350°F.

**2.** Making sure the butter is soft, cream the butter and honey together, beating well. Add the vanilla extract and continue to mix well.

**3.** Whisk together the dry ingredients, then add the mixture to the liquids and stir until there are no dry spots.

**4.** Butter a cookie sheet, or use wax or parchment paper. Use a small ice cream scoop (dipped in water to prevent the batter from sticking) to make uniformly sized balls or roll the batter into balls a little smaller than a golf ball. Place the balls on the cookie sheet and flatten, using the flat bottom of a utensil handle to create an indentation for the filling. If necessary, flatten the balls a little more with palm of your hand. Cookies should be 1½ inches to 2 inches across.

**5.** Bake for about 15 to 20 minutes, or until the cookies begin to brown around the edges.

**6.** Place the cookies on a rack to cool. Fill the indentations with your choice of ingredients, such as blueberries or raspberries mixed with maple syrup and thickened with arrowroot.

**GMB Tip:** *Make your own pecan meal by grinding fresh pecans in a food processor until it is the consistency of meal. For a yummy sandwich cookie, flatten cookies to ¼ inch thick and bake for 15 minutes or less. Place two cookies together with cream cheese or chocolate icing. If pressed for time, use an all-fruit, naturally sweetened jam or jelly spread for the filling.*

# ENERGY BARS

¼ cup (½ stick) unsalted butter, plus additional for greasing pan

1 cup raisins

¼ cup apple juice, milk, or water

2 teaspoons vanilla extract

2¼ cups oat, rye, or quinoa flakes

1 cup chopped nuts

2 teaspoons cinnamon

½ teaspoon sea salt

2 eggs, lightly whisked

⅓ cup honey

## Rebecca Wood

**WHEAT-FREE**

**Makes 8 bars**

*Here's a delicious power bar that really gives energy. The eggs and nuts make it protein-rich and the other quality ingredients provide flavor, nutrients, and satisfaction. May you be well nourished.—Rebecca*

**1.** Preheat the oven to 350°F. Lightly butter an 8×8-inch pan, or line it with parchment paper.

**2.** Place the raisins in a small bowl and stir in the apple juice (or other liquid) and vanilla extract. Set the bowl aside for 20 minutes to allow the raisins to plump.

**3.** Melt the butter in a large sauté pan over medium heat. Add the flakes and nuts and sauté, stirring constantly, for 3 to 4 minutes, or until the nuts are aromatic and a shade darker. Stir in the cinnamon and salt and sauté for an additional minute. Pour the contents into a large bowl.

**4.** Stir the eggs and honey into the raisin mixture. Pour the wet ingredients into the dry ingredients and stir until uniformly blended.

**5.** Spread the mixture into the prepared pan and bake for 30 minutes, or until golden and pulling away from the edge of the pan. Invert onto a rack to cool. Cut into bars. The energy bars will keep for 1 week.

# BLACKBERRY TART

1 9-inch piecrust (see page 125 or 127)

CUSTARD

4 egg yolks

½ cup minus 1 tablespoon maple syrup

¼ cup all-purpose flour

2 cups whole milk

¼ teaspoon pure vanilla extract

TOPPING

8 cups blackberries

¾ cup blackberry or raspberry all-fruit jam

**GMB Tip:** *This calls for a LOT of blackberries. If you don't have a large quantity of fruit, the top layer of puréed fruit does not have to be as thick— the custard is delicious even with just berries on top.*

**Makes one 9-inch tart**

*This is a classic European-style tart. It takes time and effort, but is a wonderful and beautiful way to use the tastiest berries of summer for a very special dessert, perfect at any summer celebration.—GMB*

**1.** In a glass or metal bowl, beat the egg yolks and maple syrup together until pale and foamy. Pour the mixture into the top of a double boiler. **Note:** *To create a double boiler, place the bowl on top of a pot filled with water. The bowl must be able to sit on top of the pot without falling into the water, so choose the sizes of the pot and bowl accordingly.*

**2.** Put a tablespoon or two of the egg mixture into a small bowl. Gradually add the flour and stir until well mixed. Add this mixture back into the original egg mixture.

**3.** In a small saucepan, bring the milk just to the boiling point.

**4.** Temper the eggs to prevent them from cooking by pouring a little of the hot milk into the egg mixture and stirring. Pour the remainder of the hot milk into the egg mixture. Heat in a double boiler on low heat, stirring constantly, for 4 to 5 minutes, or until thick. Add the vanilla extract.

**5.** Pour the custard into a bowl, cover, and chill in the refrigerator for several hours.

**6.** To make the topping, set aside 2 to 3 cups of the choicest blackberries. Purée the remaining berries in a food processor. Pour the purée into a bowl, add the jam, and mix until blended (this should be very thick). Chill.

**7.** Bake the piecrust and let it cool.

**8.** To assemble the tart, pour the chilled custard into the cooled piecrust, then pour the chilled blackberry mixture over the custard. Chill for several hours.

**9.** Decorate with the remaining blackberries and the mint leaves.

# FABULOUS FRUIT CRISP

## TOPPING

- 2 cups rolled oats
- ½ cup spelt flour
- ½ cup cornmeal
- 1 cup walnuts, chopped
- ½ teaspoon sea salt
- ½ cup safflower oil
- ½ cup brown rice syrup or maple syrup
- 1 teaspoon vanilla extract

## FILLING

- 1 to 2 cups fruit juice
- Pinch of sea salt
- 1 heaping tablespoon kuzu (or arrowroot), diluted in about 2 tablespoons cold water
- 3 to 4 apples, cubed
- 1 pint raspberries
- 1 pint blueberries
- 1 tablespoon brown rice syrup or maple syrup

**GMB Tip:** *To make this wheat-free, use ½ cup of oat flour instead of the spelt.*

### Melanie Waxman

**DAIRY-FREE**

**Serves 6 to 8**

*Every Sunday after church, my family had a big sit-down dinner. During the summer, we had the same thing every week: fried chicken, rice and gravy, green beans, and—fruit crisp! The fruit varied from one part of the season to the next, depending on what was available. Blackberries, blueberries, raspberries, peaches, and apples all made it into Mom's crisp. This recipe is proof that even if you give up refined sugar, you don't have to give up a dessert like this. Melanie did a really great job of mixing liquid sweeteners to get a truly crisp topping! —GMB*

**1.** Preheat the oven to 350°F.

**2.** To make the topping, in a skillet over medium heat, stir together the oats, flour, and cornmeal. Dry-roast the mixture for 5 minutes.

**3.** Place the roasted ingredients in a mixing bowl. Add the nuts and salt. Set the bowl aside.

**4.** Meanwhile, whip together the oil, rice syrup, and vanilla extract. Add the wet ingredients to the dry mixture. Mix well. Set the bowl aside.

**5.** To make the filling, in a saucepan over medium heat, combine the juice, sea salt, and diluted kuzu (or arrowroot). Heat and stir until the mixture is thick.

**6.** Add the rice syrup and mix gently.

**7.** Place the fruit and berries in a baking dish. Pour the syrup mixture over the fruit.

**8.** Sprinkle the topping over the fruit and bake for about 30 minutes. Cool, then serve.

# HUCKLEBERRY SOUR CREAM PIE

1 cup sour cream

2 tablespoons flour

½ cup maple syrup

¼ cup brown rice syrup

1 organic egg, beaten

1 teaspoon vanilla extract

¼ teaspoon salt

2½ cups berries

1 recipe graham cracker crust (see page 78) or pastry crust (see page 125)

TOPPING

3 tablespoons flour

3 tablespoons rolled oats

3 tablespoons honey

3 tablespoons butter

1 teaspoon cinnamon

3 tablespoons chopped pecans

**Makes one 9-inch pie**

*This was a favorite huckleberry dessert while living in Montana. It's fast and fantastic. It's best, of course, if you pick your own huckleberries, go straight home, and bake them into this delicious, cool summer pie. It's still fabulous even if you have to buy the berries. This is also a great recipe for using other summer berries such as blackberries, blueberries, or boysenberries.—GMB*

**1.** Preheat the oven to 350°F.

**2.** In a mixing bowl, beat together the sour cream, flour, syrups, egg, vanilla extract, and salt until smooth. Fold in the washed berries.

**3.** Pour the berry mixture into the crust and bake for 25 minutes.

**4.** While the pie is baking, mix together all the topping ingredients until the mixture resembles coarse crumbs (clumps are okay). Sprinkle the topping over the pie.

**5.** Bake another 15 to 35 minutes, or until the pie is set. Sometimes this takes up to an hour to cook. Watch the crust—you may need to cover it with strips of foil to prevent burning.

**6.** Chill several hours before serving.

**GMB Tip:** *This is really better the next day, if you can wait that long! It's also fine to substitute plain yogurt or low-fat sour cream to cut calories.*

# CHERRY PIE FILLING in BUCKWHEAT CREPES

CHERRY PIE FILLING

4 cups cherries, pitted and halved

½ cup Eden Organic apple juice, or a combination of cherry and apple juices

Pinch of Eden Organic sea salt

1 tablespoon Eden Organic barley malt syrup

1½ tablespoons organic maple syrup

1 tablespoon Eden Organic kuzu root starch (or 1 tablespoon arrowroot), dissolved in 2 tablespoons cold water

**Eden Foods (filling) and Green Market Bakers (crepes)**

**Serves 3 to 4**

*The buckwheat and cherries in this make a delightfully unusual combination. This same pie filling can be used in a regular piecrust.*
*—GMB*

**1.** Place the cherries, juice(s), salt, and syrups in a saucepan. Bring to a boil, cover, and simmer 10 minutes, or until cherries are soft.

**2.** Add the dissolved kuzu (or arrowroot), stirring constantly until the mixture is thick.

> **GMB Tip:** *To save time, buy frozen or canned cherries, making sure to read the label and get cherries in water, NOT cherries in sugar water. This filling is great in a graham cracker crust and topped with naturally sweetened whipped cream. Or serve it over Volcanic Nectar's New York–style Cheesecake (see page 78).*

# BUCKWHEAT CREPES

¼ cup (½ stick) unsalted butter

2 cups milk

1 tablespoon honey

Pinch of salt

1 cup buckwheat flour

¼ cup unbleached all-purpose flour

1 tablespoon safflower oil

3 eggs

½ cup local beer

**1.** Place the butter, milk, honey, and salt into a saucepan and heat until the butter is melted.

**2.** Place the two flours in a large mixing bowl. Make a well in the center and add the oil and eggs. Mix with a whisk until thick, then add the warm milk mixture, a little at a time, until 1 cup has been added. The mixture should be smooth and thick. Slowly add the remaining milk while whisking constantly. Add the beer and combine.

**3.** Chill the batter at least 2 hours, though overnight is preferable. Heat a crepe pan or a small nonstick pan over medium-high heat. Rub the pan with butter and pour about an ounce of crepe batter into the pan, swirling it so that the batter is thin and evenly coats the bottom of the pan. When the bottom of the crepe reaches a nice golden brown color, use a thin spatula to flip it over and cook for about another minute. Turn the crepe out onto a piece of wax paper or parchment paper while cooking the rest.

**4.** To serve, place one crepe on a plate, pour a generous amount of cherry pie filling down the center, and roll it up.

**GMB Tip:** *Try these crepes with Melissa Breyer's Lemon Curd Tart Filling (page 173) or Carol Ann Wasserman's Chocolate Ganache (see Chocolate Cupcakes with Dark Chocolate Ganache Frosting on pages 118–119), or simply fresh fruit sweetened with maple syrup. Buckwheat crepes are often filled with savory fillings as well.*

# BLUEBERRY AND CORN SKILLET BREAD

4 tablespoons butter, divided

¾ cup stone-ground cornmeal

1 cup stone-ground whole wheat flour

2 teaspoons baking powder

½ teaspoon salt

1 cup blueberries, fresh or frozen

¾ cup milk

¼ cup raw honey

1 large egg

**Linda Johnson and Michael Johnson**

**Makes one 8-inch or two 6-inch rounds**

*We like this skillet bread because it is a sweet cornbread that can be served for breakfast. Plus, guests love it! Except for the baking powder, all ingredients can be found locally in most communities.—Linda and Michael*

**1.** Preheat the oven to 350°F.

**2.** Melt 2 tablespoons of butter in an 8-inch cast-iron pan (or ovenproof skillet) or melt 1 tablespoon of butter in a 6-inch cast-iron pan (or ovenproof skillet). Repeat with another 6-inch pan.

**3.** Combine the dry ingredients in a large mixing bowl. Add the blueberries.

**4.** In a separate bowl, combine the milk, honey, and egg. **Note:** *If you grease the measuring cup with butter before measuring the honey, the honey slides right out, making both measuring and cleaning up much easier.* Melt the remaining 2 tablespoons of butter and add to the milk mixture.

**5.** Fold the wet ingredients into the dry ingredients. Add the melted butter to the batter.

**6.** Pour the batter into the pan(s) and bake for 25 to 35 minutes, or until a toothpick inserted in the center comes out clean. These skillet breads are great right out of the oven.

# BLUEBERRY MUFFINS

7 tablespoons unsalted butter, at room temperature

⅓ cup brown rice syrup

⅓ cup plus 2 tablespoons maple syrup

2 large eggs

2¼ cups unbleached all-purpose flour

4 teaspoons baking powder

½ teaspoon salt

¾ cup plus 1 tablespoon whole milk

1½ teaspoons vanilla extract

1½ cups blueberries, fresh or frozen

TOPPING

2 tablespoons unbleached all-purpose flour

2 tablespoons maple sugar

¼ teaspoon cinnamon

2 tablespoons cold butter

**Note:** *These freeze really well.*

**Makes 12 large muffins**

*These sweet blueberry muffins are light and fluffy, and full of delicious, juicy blueberries. They work just as well if you use frozen berries, making this a super year-round recipe. The topping is the "icing on the cake," but can be left off if you don't have maple sugar. —GMB*

**1.** Preheat the oven to 350°F. Butter the muffin cups or use paper liners.

**2.** Cream together the butter, syrups, and eggs until well blended.

**3.** In a separate bowl, mix together the dry ingredients.

**4.** Add the dry ingredients to the butter mixture in two batches, alternating with the milk and vanilla extract.

**5.** Gently fold in the blueberries. Spoon the batter into the muffin cups.

**6.** To make the topping, cut the butter into the other ingredients until the mixture resembles crumbs. Sprinkle each muffin with the topping.

**7.** Bake 20 to 25 minutes, or until the top of a muffin springs back when gently poked.

**8.** Let the muffins cool in the pan for 5 minutes, then remove and serve them warm or cold.

# FIG AND BLUEBERRY SCONES

2 cups unbleached all-purpose flour

1 tablespoon baking powder

½ teaspoon salt

7 tablespoons unsalted cold butter, plus 2 tablespoons for honey butter

1 large egg

⅓ cup raw honey, plus 3 tablespoons for honey butter

½ cup organic heavy cream

1 cup (total) mixture of fresh figs, quartered, and blueberries, fresh or frozen

**Makes 8 scones**

*These scones are moist and crumbly and are great to serve for brunch or afternoon tea. Though we offer the recipe using blueberries and figs, you can easily substitute with the berry or fruit of your choice—just use whatever is available.—GMB*

**1.** Preheat the oven to 425°F.

**2.** Mix the flour, baking powder, and salt together in a bowl. Using a cheese grater, grate the very cold butter into the flour mixture. Put this bowl in the freezer while whisking the egg, honey, and cream together in a separate bowl until fully blended.

**3.** Take the flour bowl from the freezer, add the blueberries and figs, and toss the fruit to coat.

**4.** Add the liquids to the fruit mixture and form the dough into a ball. If the dough is not coming together, add extra cream (be sure it's cold!). The less you work the dough, the better.

**5.** Turn the dough out onto a floured surface and form it into a circle about 8 inches in diameter. Cut the dough into 8 triangular slices (like pizza or pie). Place the individual scones on an ungreased cookie sheet. Bake for 12 to 15 minutes, or until the scones are lightly browned.

**6.** While the scones are baking, heat the remaining honey and butter in a saucepan just until the butter is melted. Do not let it boil. As soon as you take the scones out of the oven, brush them with the honey butter.

# ZUCCHINI SPICE MUFFINS

2 cups (8 ounces) walnuts or pecans

2 cups stone-ground unbleached all-purpose flour

½ cup maple sugar

1 teaspoon baking soda

1 teaspoon baking powder

1 teaspoon cinnamon

1 teaspoon fine sea salt

¼ teaspoon freshly ground white pepper

½ cup cold-pressed, light tasting olive oil

½ cup raw, unfiltered local honey

1 teaspoon vanilla extract

½ tablespoon freshly grated ginger

2 large eggs, beaten

1¼ pounds zucchini, peeled and shredded (about 4 cups)

**GMB Tip:** *Try this recipe with maple syrup instead of maple sugar, using ½ cup maple syrup and adding ½ tablespoon of arrowroot to the flour. It is superb.*

**Michelle McKenzie**

**Makes 18 muffins**

*These muffins are fast, nutritious, and delicious! Using two different sweeteners here, maple sugar and honey, adds dimension and prevents either ingredient from overpowering the other flavors. Perfect for a light Sunday brunch.—Michelle*

**1.** Preheat the oven to 350°F. Line the muffin cups with paper liners.

**2.** Spread the nuts on a large-rimmed baking sheet lined with parchment paper and bake about 7 minutes, until toasted. While the nuts are still warm, fold them into a clean kitchen towel and lightly rub to remove their bitter skins. Let the nuts cool, then coarsely chop them.

**3.** Sift the flour, maple sugar, baking soda, baking powder, cinnamon, salt, and white pepper into a medium bowl; whisk the ingredients to combine.

**4.** In a large bowl, whisk together the olive oil, honey, vanilla extract, grated ginger, and eggs.

**5.** Gather the zucchini into a cheesecloth or a clean towel and squeeze out the moisture. Stir the nuts and the zucchini into the wet ingredients. Add the dry ingredients in small batches until everything is thoroughly incorporated.

**6.** Using an ice cream scoop, scoop the batter into the lined muffin cups. Bake 23 to 27 minutes, rotating the pan halfway through, until the muffins are golden and a toothpick inserted into the center of a muffin comes out clean. Transfer the muffins to a wire rack and let them cool to room temperature.

# GOAT CHEESE AND GREEN GARLIC FLAN

**CRUST**

- 4 ounces goat cheese
- ¼ cup bread crumbs
- 1 tablespoon finely chopped herbs

**FILLING**

- 1 tablespoon olive oil
- 1 cup green garlic (or fresh onions and shallots), thinly sliced on bias
- 4 egg yolks plus 6 whole eggs
- 1 quart fresh goat's milk (or 3 cups half-and-half and 1 cup buttermilk)
- 3 tablespoons locust or acacia honey (or any light-colored honey)
- ¼ cup finely chopped fresh herbs (we used chervil, fennel fronds, dill, and thyme)
- 2 teaspoons fine sea salt
- 4 to 6 grinds of white pepper (or to taste)
- Dash of nutmeg and chili powder (optional)

### Mark Haskell

**Makes 6–8 ramekins**

*One weekend during the height of spring, I was invited to a cook's nirvana in Douglasville, Georgia, at Skip and Cookie Glover's organic farm. They had fields full of green garlic, fresh eggs, baby beets, and every herb imaginable, and promised that they could get me any other wonderful ingredient that Georgia farmers produce—locust honey, pecans, local goat's milk, and much more. I was inspired to put together this farm-fresh flan. It includes a wide array of flavors and colors from the great ingredients that were available in that season and place.—Mark*

**1.** Preheat the oven to 350°F. In a small bowl, mix together all the ingredients for the crust. Set aside.

**2.** Sauté the green garlic in a pan with the oil and a little salt and pepper, just long enough to soften it but not brown. Set aside.

**3.** Mix the eggs and milk until well blended, then add the other ingredients, including the garlic.

**4.** Butter the sides and bottoms of the ramekins, then coat the bottoms with the crust mixture.

**5.** Pour the filling mixture into the ramekins, stopping a half-inch below the top. Place all the ramekins in a large baking pan with high sides.

**6.** Pour hot water into pan, to just above halfway up the side of the ramekins. Loosely cover the whole pan with aluminum foil, but don't seal the edges.

**7.** Turning the pan around once while cooking, bake 20 to 25 minutes, or until the custard becomes firm throughout. Remove from the oven and cool.

**8.** To serve, use the tip of a knife and gently circle the edge of the flan to loosen. Invert onto a plate and serve with a salad, soup, or anything you like.

# SWEET CORN TART

## Meredith McCarty

**DAIRY-FREE**

**Serves 10**

FILLING

1 pound fresh tofu, medium or firm (not soft or extra-firm)

Kernels from 3 ears of sweet yellow corn

½ teaspoon sea salt or 1 tablespoon umeboshi paste (or ¼ teaspoon sea salt *and* ½ tablespoon umeboshi paste)

Up to ¼ cup water (none needed if using medium tofu)

¼ cup finely chopped basil (or dill)

¼ cup finely chopped green onions (or chives)

¼ teaspoon turmeric (optional)

PASTRY

½ cup whole wheat pastry flour

½ cup unbleached white pastry flour

Pinch of sea salt

2 tablespoons light vegetable oil (such as Spectrum walnut)

Up to 3 tablespoons water

*Umeboshi is a pickled, salted plum used for both culinary and medicinal purposes and is available in the macrobiotic section of natural food stores. Ancient Japanese samurai, who had active, outdoor lifestyles, used it to avoid dysentery when drinking from streams and eating wild foods. Served atop rice for breakfast at Japanese inns today, umeboshi plums are alkalinizing to the blood, in addition to having antibacterial, antiviral, and antifungal properties. This filling turns golden yellow with baking.—Meredith*

**1.** Preheat the oven to 400°F.

**2.** To make the filling, purée the tofu and corn with the salt or umeboshi paste until creamy and smooth. Add the water gradually (only if needed) to blend. Fold in the basil (or dill), green onions (or chives), and turmeric (if using).

**3.** To make the pastry, mix the dry ingredients, stir in the oil, then add water as needed to form a smooth, moist dough. Handle the dough as little as possible. Transfer to a floured sheet of wax paper. Sprinkle the dough with flour and place another sheet of wax paper on top. Roll the dough out thin and transfer it to the tart pan. Cut off the pastry a finger's width away from the outer edge and fold it over toward the inside. Press the edge to make a rim.

**4.** Fill and bake for about 60 minutes, or until the surface is a bright golden yellow. For a greater sheen, lightly brush the pastry crust with a little oil before baking.

# PESTO PIZZA
## WITH GOAT CHEESE AND FIGS

1 12-inch pizza shell
   or dough

1 4-ounce jar of Hope's
   Gardens Basil Pesto
   (or ⅔ cup homemade,
   recipe follows)

12 figs, halved

8 medallions (about
   4 ounces) goat cheese

   Salt and pepper

### Hope's Gardens

**Serves 4**

*We put some serrano ham on this pizza and it was literally one of the best things we've ever tasted (you could also use prosciutto). The combination of the sweet figs and the salty ham with the pesto and goat cheese was amazing. If you purchase the pizza crust ready-made, you can make this dish as an appetizer or as a main dish in about 15 minutes. It is VERY impressive.—GMB*

**1.** Preheat the oven or grill to 450°F.

**2.** Roll out the pizza dough or take a pizza shell and spread a layer of Hope's Gardens pesto (or the homemade pesto) on top.

**3.** Place the goat cheese and scatter the fig halves on top of the pesto. Season with salt and pepper.

**4.** Bake for 10 to 12 minutes, or until the crust is golden brown.

# PESTO

2 cups packed basil leaves

⅓ cup pine nuts

½ cup extra virgin olive oil

2 to 3 garlic cloves (depending on clove size and personal preference)

½ cup Parmesan cheese

**GMB Tip:** *This pesto has a strong garlic flavor, so adjust the amount of garlic according to taste.*

*Not only is this pesto great on the pizza featured on the previous page, it is also fabulous on pasta or bruschetta.—GMB*

**1.** Place the basil leaves in a food processor, pulsing several times. Add the pine nuts and garlic, pulsing again until the ingredients are well chopped.

**2.** As the food processor runs continuously, add a slow stream of olive oil to blend all the ingredients.

**3.** Turn off the food processor, then add the Parmesan cheese and process again until everything is well blended.

# TOMATO BREAD

1 pound or more of tomatoes (or 1½ to 2 cups canned tomato sauce)

4 cups bread flour, plus additional as needed

2 tablespoons active dry yeast

3 teaspoons salt

4 tablespoons (½ stick) unsalted butter, melted (plus additional for bowl) or 4 tablespoons olive oil (plus additional for bowl)

2 cups breadcrumbs (if making rolls)

**Amy Besa and Romy Dorotan**
**Makes 1 loaf or 18 rolls**

*Romy tested two types of loaves: one with red tomato purée and butter, and the other with yellow tomato purée and olive oil. Both are quite nice. The red tomato version is richer and the yellow tomato bread has a beautiful olive flavor that goes well with Italian dishes. —Amy*

**TO MAKE THE TOMATO PURÉE**

**1.** Bring a large pot of water to a boil over high heat and fill a large mixing bowl with water and ice. Using a paring knife, make a small X in the bottom of each tomato. Lower the tomatoes into the boiling water, two at a time, and blanch until the skin at the bottom of the tomato begins to curl, about 30 seconds. Using a slotted spoon, immediately transfer the tomatoes to the ice water to cool. Repeat until all the tomatoes have been blanched.

**2.** When the tomatoes are cool enough to handle, remove the skins by hand or with a paring knife. Slice the tomatoes in half, remove and discard the seeds, and chop the flesh into chunks. Place the tomatoes in a blender and purée until smooth, then strain the purée through a medium-mesh strainer set over a bowl.

**TO MAKE THE DOUGH**

**1.** Mix the yeast with 1½ to 2 cups of the puréed tomatoes and let the mixture stand about 5 minutes, or until it starts to bubble.

**2.** In the bowl of a standing electric mixer fitted with the paddle attachment, combine half the bread flour with the tomato purée mixture and salt, and mix to form a smooth batter. Blend in the butter (or olive oil).

**3.** Change the mixer attachment to the dough hook. With the hook in motion, add the remaining bread flour, ½ cup at a time, until the dough forms into a rough mass that easily pulls away from the sides of the bowl.

### TO MAKE A LOAF

**1.** Transfer the dough to a large buttered bowl and cover it with plastic wrap. Place the covered bowl in a warm, draft-free spot and let it rise about 1 hour, or until doubled in bulk.

**2.** Butter a 9½×5½×2½-inch pan.

**3.** On a floured surface, roll the dough into a log that fits the pan. Place the dough into the pan and cover it with buttered plastic wrap. Let it rise until the dough reaches a half inch over the top of the pan (about 1 hour).

**4.** Preheat the oven to 400°F.

**5.** Bake for 35 minutes. Remove the bread from the pan and cool on a wire rack. Serve warm or at room temperature.

### TO MAKE ROLLS

**1.** Pour the breadcrumbs into a shallow dish. Follow the loaf recipe up to step 3.

**2.** Punch the dough down once more and cut it in half. Working with half the dough at a time, form about 18 total rolls (weighing 2 ounces each). Roll the balls in the breadcrumbs to coat and place them on the baking sheet. Cover loosely with a damp kitchen towel and let the rolls rise for 30 minutes.

**3.** During the final rising, preheat the oven to 400°F. Sprinkle the rolls with more bread crumbs and transfer them to the oven. Bake for 20 to 25 minutes, or until the rolls are lightly browned and hard on the bottom. Cool the rolls on wire racks. Serve warm or at room temperature.

# TOMATO, GOAT CHEESE, AND BASIL CORNBREAD

6 tablespoons butter

4 small green onions, white parts only, chopped

2½ tablespoons chopped basil

1½ cups unbleached flour

1 cup stone-ground cornmeal

3½ teaspoons baking powder

½ teaspoon salt

1¼ cups milk

2 large eggs

¼ cup crumbled goat cheese (plain or flavored)

2 plum tomatoes

4 to 6 whole basil leaves

**Makes 4 small loaves**

*This is a great little cornbread with a beautiful center of red tomato, white cheese, and green basil. Unlike the previous Tomato Bread recipe, which incorporates tomato juice into the batter, here the tomatoes are left in chunks and baked into the center. It makes a good accompaniment for a summer salad, or it can be sliced and reheated for an interesting appetizer.—GMB*

**1.** Preheat the oven to 400°F.

**2.** Grease four small loaf pans with olive oil.

**3.** Melt 6 tablespoons of butter in a frying pan. Add the chopped green onions and sauté them until soft. Add the chopped basil and turn off the heat.

**4.** In a large bowl, mix the unbleached flour, cornmeal, baking powder, and salt. In a separate bowl, mix the eggs and milk with the onion mixture. Make a well in the dry ingredients and add the egg mixture, stirring until just blended. Do not overmix.

**5.** Divide half the batter among the four loaf pans.

**6.** Chop the tomatoes into small chunks. Place 1 tablespoon of chopped tomatoes lengthwise down the center of the batter in each pan. Sprinkle about 1 tablespoon of goat cheese on top of the tomatoes, topped by 1 to 2 small whole basil leaves. Finish with the remaining batter.

**7.** Bake for about 20 minutes, or until golden brown.

**8.** Remove the bread from the pans and cool on a wire rack. Just before serving, cut each loaf into ½-inch slices, place on a cookie sheet, and toast in the oven. Serve hot.

# YELLOW SQUASH AND SUN-DRIED TOMATO "QUICHE"

1 tablespoon olive oil

1 large yellow onion, sliced very thin

1½ cups (6 ounces) shredded mozzarella

½ cup (1 ounce) freshly grated Parmesan cheese, divided

2 teaspoons fresh thyme leaves

¼ cup finely minced green onions, white and light green parts

1 cup (about 3 ounces) julienned sun-dried tomatoes in oil, drained

½ cup finely julienned basil

1 medium yellow squash

3 extra-large eggs

1 cup half-and-half

¼ teaspoon salt

**Rozanne Gold**

Serves 6–8

*This is one fantastic recipe using the bounty of summer that is not only delicious, but colorful and beautiful too. It is a "crustless quiche," meaning it is quick and easy to make—and saves on extra calories.*
*—GMB*

**1.** Preheat the oven to 400°F.

**2.** Drizzle the olive oil in an 8-inch metal pie tin. Line the bottom of the pie tin with the onions to make a thin layer. Scatter the mozzarella evenly over the onion layer. Sprinkle with 6 tablespoons of the Parmesan, plus the thyme, green onions, sun-dried tomatoes, and basil.

**3.** Cut the yellow squash into very thin rounds and place them in the pie tin in concentric circles ¼ inch apart.

**4.** Beat together the eggs, half-and-half, and salt until the mixture is thoroughly blended. Pour the mixture into the tin, and sprinkle with the remaining 2 tablespoons Parmesan.

**5.** Bake 35 minutes, or until the top is golden brown. Serve warm or at room temperature.

**GMB Tip:** *Sauteeing the onions for a few minutes before putting them in the pie tin makes for an even sweeter quiche.*

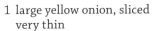

# VEGETABLE FRITTATA WITH SUMMER SQUASH, SUMMER ONION, AND FRESH BASIL

1 white onion with green stem, sliced (keep sliced green stem for separate use)

3 tablespoons butter or olive oil

2 summer squashes, cut in half lengthwise, sliced into half-moons

3 eggs

½ cup cream or half-and-half

Salt and pepper

Pinch or grating of nutmeg

½ cup grated or crumbled local cheese

½ bunch basil leaves, cut into ribbons

**Jessica Prentice**
*Full Moon Feast* (Chelsea Green Publishing, 2006)
**Serves 2 to 4**

*This is a fabulous way to use farm-fresh eggs and a variety of summer vegetables. It is a great basic recipe, flexible enough to use for whatever you have on hand. If you use local butter, you can probably make this entirely from local ingredients.—GMB*

**1.** In a heavy-bottomed pan over medium-high heat, sauté the onions in the butter or olive oil for a few minutes, until the onions are translucent.

**2.** Add the summer squash and sauté until tender.

**3.** Mix together the eggs and cream in a bowl. Add salt (be generous—start with a teaspoon and then add more if needed), fresh pepper, and nutmeg.

**4.** Reduce the heat and pour the eggs over the sautéed vegetables. Add the cheese, onion greens, and half the basil and cover.

**5.** Cook the frittata over low heat until just set. You can also bake it in the oven, preheated to 300°F, to finish cooking.

**6.** Slice and serve with more basil on top.

**Jessica's variations:** *(1) Add sliced or diced Gypsy peppers to the sauté. (2) Lay sliced tomatoes on the top of the frittata. (3) Add fresh corn kernels to the sauté. (4) Replace basil with another fresh herb such as marjoram, green onions, or chives.*

# BLUEBERRY GINGER SAUCE

1 pint fresh or frozen
blueberries

¼ cup maple syrup*

1 tablespoon cornstarch

½ teaspoon dried ginger

⅓ cup water

* original recipe called for
¼ cup sugar

**U.S. Highbush Blueberry Council**

**Makes 1½ cups**

*What a great sauce for all kinds of things! It is super over ice cream or on top of a plain cake (such as Martha Foose's Maple Sugar Angel Food Cake (page 157), or Debra Lynn Dadd's All-Organic Special Occasion Cake (page 76). You can also pour it over waffles or pancakes. You can substitute other berries, such as raspberries or blackberries, for the blueberries.—GMB*

**1.** In a large saucepan over medium-high heat, bring all the ingredients to a boil. Cook, stirring constantly, about 1 minute, or until sauce thickens.

# RED PLUM BASIL RELISH

5 medium red plums, pitted and thinly sliced

⅓ cup basil chiffonade

1 tablespoon honey

1 tablespoon fresh lemon juice

1 tablespoon extra virgin olive oil

Kosher salt and freshly ground black pepper

**Tom Douglas**

**Serves 4 to 6**

*This simple relish is delicious with grilled fish, chicken, or pork, and it's a great way to feature perfectly ripe summer fruit. Instead of red plums, you could substitute a similar quantity of purple plums, nectarines, or peeled peaches.—Tom*

**1.** In a large bowl, combine all the ingredients. Serve at room temperature.

**GMB Tip:** *Chiffonade is a French cutting technique in which herbs or leafy green vegetables (such as spinach and basil) are cut into long, thin strips. This is generally accomplished by stacking leaves, rolling them tightly, then cutting across the rolled leaves with a sharp knife, producing fine ribbons approximately ¼ inch wide.*

# SIMPSON COUNTY WATERMELON SORBET

⅔ cup boiling water

⅔ cup local honey

4 cups fresh watermelon, seeded

2 tablespoons lemon juice

**GMB Tip:** *Be sure that the ice cream maker container is frozen and that the fruit and honey purée is very cold before you begin cranking!*

**David Romines**

**Makes about 1 quart**

*This is a very sweet, light dessert and a great way to use summer watermelons.—GMB*

**1.** In a small bowl, pour the boiling water over the honey and stir until dissolved.

**2.** Cover and chill.

**3.** Purée the fruit and run through a sieve, if necessary. Combine the fruit with the honey syrup.

**4.** Freeze in an ice cream maker according to the manufacturer's directions.

Almonds
Apples
Butternut squash
Cranberries
Figs
Garlic
Ginger
Grapes
Mushrooms
Onions
Pears
Pecans
Persimmons
Pumpkins
Spinach
Sweet potatoes
Walnuts
Winter squash

# FALL

AN APPLE TREE STOOD IN THE CENTER OF THE BACKYARD WHERE I GREW up, right outside Atlanta. Gnarled and tough-skinned, it was an old tree, left over from the farming days of earlier decades. The apples were green and tart and usually hard as a rock, but they made the most delicious pies in the world. Late summer and early fall were the days of harvest, and my mother, who grew up during the Depression and never really got over it, was determined to use every bit of apple she could salvage from that tree.

I was usually the one sent out during the crisp autumn days to bring back as many ripe apples as I could find. Braving the yellow jackets that swarmed over the ground and who were feasting on those few rare apples that managed to escape my mother's grasp, I sidled up to the tree, threw a leg over the lowest limb, and pulled myself up so that I was sitting in the tree. We rarely bothered to prune, and the branches were thick and intertwined, making climbing difficult, but I slithered and scraped my way up until I could reach the biggest, ripest apples on the tree.

Nothing in the world tasted better to me during those cool fall nights than my mother's "live apple pie," as my Daddy used to call it. It was his way of saying that the pie was made from "live" apples—fresh, as local and as seasonal as we could get, and as alive as any I've ever had since. Mom had no problem using sugar—she added enough to make the tart apples release the sweetness in their juice. Fortunately, we found that maple syrup and honey will do just about the same thing, with healthier results.

Of course, apples are just the tip of the produce iceberg in fall. Autumn is the season for gathering and storing and making the most of what the garden and orchard have to offer. For a traditional treat, try Debra Lynn Dadd's Pumpkin Pie and Custard (page 130). For tradition with a twist, try Sabrina Model-Carlberg's recipe for Butternut Squash Cake with Cream Cheese Frosting (page 117). If you're in the mood to use some unconventional ingredients, make Charles Sanders's great Persimmon Bread (page 142), or try your hand at making Sorghum Gingerbread (page 140).

Whatever you decide to bake this fall, I'm sure you're going to want to make a "live" apple pie—or pear, or whatever "live" things you can find close to home. You may not want to climb the tree to get them—but then again, maybe you will. Happy harvest!

• • • • • • •

## Choosing Produce

**APPLES** Choose apples that are firm, with no bad spots. The old adage "one bad apple spoils the barrel" is based on truth. Apples stored in the refrigerator in a ventilated plastic bag or container will generally last for a couple of months. Use freshly cut apples as quickly as you can, as they tend to turn brown when exposed to the air. If you have to wait to serve or use cut apples, sprinkle them with a bit of lemon juice. You can also freeze peeled and sliced apples to use in pies, cakes, or applesauce later.

**FIGS** Figs, fresh or dried, are wonderful for baking. Fresh figs have a very short season, so make the most of them. They bruise easily, so handle carefully. If you pick slightly firm ones and put them in an airtight container, they last for up to a week in the refrigerator. When cutting figs, use a sharp knife or kitchen scissors. If the utensil gets sticky, clean it off before you continue cutting, to keep a sharper cut on the blade and prevent tearing of the fruit.

Dried figs can be used for a variety of purposes. They are relatively easy to dry at home with a dehydrator or, with a little more effort, in a warm oven. With either method, you want to dry the figs slowly so that the inside of the fruit dries at the same rate as the outside—you want to make sure you're not trapping moisture inside the fruit. Once the figs are dry, be sure you kill any lurking bacteria either by cooking them in a 175°F oven for 10 to 15 minutes or by putting them in the freezer for at least 4 days. Properly dried figs should last for over a year.

**GRAPES** Be sure to choose grapes that are firm and plump, not wrinkled or bruised. Grapes can be stored in the refrigerator for at least a week. Red grapes are harvested only in fall and winter. Of course, whenever possible, choose local grapes. Not only do they have a smaller environmental footprint, they also tend to retain fewer pesticides, according to the Environmental Working Group tests.

ONIONS Choose onions that are firm and look crisp with no bruising. The skins should be dry and crackly and should not show any green stems or sprouts. If placed in mesh bags, onions should last in the crisper drawer of the refrigerator for several months.

PERSIMMONS There are two distinctly different kinds of persimmons grown in the United States today. The American persimmon is native to the eastern half of the country; it can be found from Florida to the New England states, and as far west as Texas. The Asian persimmon grows in warmer regions of the United States; commercially, Asian persimmons are grown in California, Florida, and, to a lesser extent, southeastern Texas.

All persimmons need to be ripe before they're eaten or used in baking. A ripe persimmon has a beautiful deep, reddish orange skin with no yellow spots and will yield to gentle pressure. If you have persimmons that are not quite ripe, place them in a paper bag with a ripe banana or apple until they are soft and ready to use.

PEARS When ripe and ready to use, pears should be slightly soft toward the stem. Yellow Bartlett pears start off light green, turning yellow as they ripen. Red Bartletts are brownish red. Bosc pears are brown. Anjou pears do not change colors as they ripen but remain either purplish red or green. Comice pears are yellow with a red blush. Seckels are smaller than other varieties and have a maroonish green skin. Choose slightly firmer pears for baking. Once pears are ripe, they can be stored in the refrigerator for up to 2 months.

PUMPKINS The best pumpkins for baking are generally marked as "pie" or "sugar" pumpkins. They are usually much smaller than jack-o-lantern pumpkins and their meat is much more tender and tasty. The meat can be puréed and used in pies, muffins, and cakes. Cut them in half and roast in the oven until the meat is tender. The best pumpkin varieties for making pies include "Winter Luxury Pie," "Small Sugar," or "Cheese."

**SWEET POTATOES** Sweet potatoes should be firm, with no wrinkling or blemishes. Odd and interesting shapes seem to be inherent to the vegetable and in no way detract from the taste (though it makes them a little more difficult to peel). Handle sweet potatoes carefully to keep from bruising them. They retain their flavor best if stored in a cool, dry place (but not in the refrigerator). If you have an excessive number of sweet potatoes and can't use them right away, slice and freeze them for later use.

Although sweet potatoes and yams are sometimes considered the same thing, they are actually quite different. Yams are a much, much larger vegetable (a single yam can sometimes weigh as much as 150 pounds!) and are rarely seen at local farmers' markets or grocery stores.

Puréed sweet potatoes are used much like pumpkin purée in breads and muffins.

**WINTER SQUASH** Winter and summer squash are completely different. Winter squash, which include acorn and butternut, will last several months if stored in a cool, dry, well-ventilated place, such as a root cellar. Place them on a thick stack of newspaper and check periodically for rot. Remove any decaying fruit. They will last much longer under these circumstances than they will in the refrigerator. However, most of us don't have access to a root cellar these days, necessitating storage in the fridge. Once the squash is cut, cover with plastic wrap and store in the refrigerator.

If you want to preserve winter squash in the freezer, cut it into pieces, cook, and cool before putting into freezer bags or containers.

Butternut squash can be used much like pumpkin in cakes, breads, and muffins.

# APPLE CAKE

CAKE

1 cup maple syrup

¾ cup brown rice syrup

1½ cups very lightly flavored olive oil

3 eggs

2 teaspoons vanilla extract

3 cups unbleached all-purpose flour

1 teaspoon baking soda

2 teaspoons cinnamon

¾ teaspoon salt

4½ to 5 cups apples, peeled and chopped, such as Granny Smith

1¼ cups coarsely chopped pecans (or walnuts)

½ cup raisins (optional)

GLAZE

¼ cup (½ stick) butter

½ cup maple syrup

½ cup heavy cream

Makes one 9×13-inch cake

*We were delighted to find out we could easily (and deliciously) substitute natural sweeteners in this cake with fantastic results. The maple syrup and apples are a fabulous combination.—GMB*

**1.** Preheat the oven to 325°F.

**2.** Measure the olive oil in a glass measuring cup and pour into a large bowl. Use the same cup to measure the syrups. Add the vanilla, and mix until well blended.

**3.** Add the eggs one at a time, mixing well after each addition.

**4.** In a separate bowl, mix together the flour, baking soda, cinnamon, and salt.

**5.** Gradually add the dry ingredients to the wet mixture, mixing well but not overmixing.

**6.** Fold in the apples and nuts (and raisins if using).

**7.** Pour into a greased and floured 9×13-inch baking pan. Bake for at least 1 hour, until a toothpick inserted into the center comes out clean.

**8.** Leave the cake in the pan as you prepare the glaze. Melt the butter in a saucepan, then add the maple syrup and stir, cooking over low heat for 2 minutes. Stir in the cream and boil for 2 minutes, stirring constantly. Remove from the heat and allow to cool slightly.

**9.** Leave the cake in the pan and poke holes all over with a fork or skewer. Pour the slightly cooled glaze over the cake, making sure to distribute it evenly.

# BUTTERNUT SQUASH CAKE
## WITH CREAM CHEESE FROSTING

### CAKE

- ⅔ cup grapeseed oil (or any mild oil)
- ¾ cup maple syrup (we like Grade B dark)
- 3 eggs
- 2 tablespoons Greek yogurt
- 1¾ cups unbleached flour
- 1½ teaspoons baking powder
- 1 teaspoon baking soda
- 2 tablespoons spices of your choice (try a combination of cinnamon, nutmeg, ginger, and cardamom)
- 1 cup cooked and mashed butternut squash (or canned unsweetened pumpkin purée)

### FROSTING

- 1 8-ounce package light cream cheese
- ¼ cup maple syrup
- 1 teaspoon molasses or dark honey

### Sabrina Model-Carlberg

Serves 8 to 10

*Butternut squash is often overlooked as an ingredient in baking, but it is a fabulously delicious ingredient and can be used just about anytime you would use pumpkin—in pies, muffins, or in this wonderful cake. It's actually easier to prepare fresh butternut squash than fresh pumpkin, and it's far more prevalent in home gardens. So warn your family—it's squash for dessert tonight! One taste and they'll be hooked.—Sabrina*

### CAKE

**1.** Preheat the oven to 350°F. Place the oil and maple syrup in a bowl and beat well for a minute or two.

**2.** Add the eggs gradually and beat well. Add the yogurt and beat a bit more.

**3.** Sift the flour, baking soda, baking powder, and spices into the bowl. Mix together, then add the butternut purée. Beat all the ingredients until just mixed.

**4.** Line a buttered 9-inch round cake pan with parchment paper. Pour the batter into the pan, then bake 40 to 45 minutes, or until a toothpick inserted into the center comes out clean.

**5.** Serve warm or cool completely. Try it with the amazing Cream Cheese Frosting.

### FROSTING

**1.** Blend all ingredients in a food processor until smooth.

# CHOCOLATE CUPCAKES WITH DARK CHOCOLATE GANACHE FROSTING

### CUPCAKES

- 1 teaspoon apple cider vinegar
- ⅔ cup unsweetened soy milk
- 1 cup whole-grain spelt flour
- ⅓ cup cocoa powder
- ½ teaspoon baking powder
- ¾ teaspoon baking soda
- ¼ teaspoon sea salt
- ¼ cup agave nectar
- ¼ cup maple syrup
- 1 cup safflower oil (or sesame or sunflower oil)
- 1½ teaspoons vanilla extract

### Carol Anne Wasserman

**DAIRY-FREE**

Makes 10 to 12 cupcakes

*This is one of my favorite treats! These cupcakes are super light, fluffy, and moist. This is an astoundingly good dessert; you won't be disappointed!—Carol Anne*

### CUPCAKES

**1.** Prepare the Dark Chocolate Ganache Frosting.

**2.** Preheat the oven to 350°F.

**3.** In a large measuring cup or small bowl, mix together the apple cider vinegar and soy milk with a fork. Let it sit for a few minutes.

**4.** In a separate bowl, combine the spelt flour, cocoa powder, baking powder, baking soda, and salt. Mix well with a wire whisk.

**5.** Beat the milk mixture again. Add the agave nectar, maple syrup, oil, and vanilla extract to the milk mixture, whisking until well combined.

**6.** Add the wet ingredients to the dry ingredients and mix with a whisk until only a few lumps remain. Do not overmix.

**7.** Spoon into 10 or 11 medium-sized muffin cups, lined with paper liners. Bake for 12 to 14 minutes, or until a toothpick inserted in the center comes out clean.

FROSTING

- 2 ounces unsweetened chocolate, in small pieces
- ¼ cup milk (or soy milk)
- ¼ cup maple syrup
- ½ pound soft tofu (half a 14-ounce package works fine)
- ¼ cup brown rice syrup
- Pinch of sea salt
- 2 teaspoons vanilla extract

**GMB Tip:** *This icing doesn't look as if it would firm up, but it will. It can also be used as a filling in pastries or mini pie shells, or on top of a plain cake such as Debra Lynn Dadd's All-Organic Special Occasion Cake (see page 76).*

## FROSTING

**1.** Heat the chocolate, milk, and maple syrup in a double boiler until the chocolate melts. Let it cool slightly.

**2.** In a blender or food processor combine the cooled chocolate mixture, tofu, brown rice syrup, sea salt, and vanilla extract. Blend until smooth, then refrigerate for several hours until firm.

# ALMOND SQUARES

½ cup almond meal

¼ teaspoon sea salt

½ cup brown rice syrup

1 cup healthy butter substitute, such as Earth Balance

1 teaspoon almond extract

1¼ cups whole wheat pastry flour

1 teaspoon baking powder

½ cup slivered almonds, lightly toasted

**Christina Pirello**

`DAIRY-FREE`

Makes 18 bars

*Easy, nutty, and delightfully satisfying. That, together with the healthful proteins and fats found in almonds, and you have yummy perfection!—Christina*

**1.** Preheat the oven to 350°F. Lightly oil a 9-inch square baking dish.

**2.** Combine the almond meal, salt, brown rice syrup, and butter substitute in a small saucepan over low heat. Cook, stirring occasionally, for about 3 minutes. Remove the pan from the heat and whisk in the almond extract. Transfer to a mixing bowl.

**3.** Whisk the flour and baking powder into the syrup mixture and stir until a spreadable batter forms. Fold in the almonds.

**4.** Spread evenly in the prepared pan and bake for 25 to 30 minutes. Remove from the oven and cool completely in the pan before slicing into 1½×3-inch bars.

# APPLE OAT PECAN DROPS

1½ cups rolled oats

1 tablespoon whole wheat flour

2 medium apples, grated

1 tablespoon oil

½ teaspoon vanilla extract

¼ cup water

½ cup raisins

¼ cup finely chopped pecans

## Schermer Pecans

**DAIRY-FREE** **LOW-FAT** **VEGAN**

Makes 20 cookies

*This is a pretty amazing recipe. It has no sweetener in it except for the apples, and is easy, vegan, low in fat, and can be easily altered to a wheat-free recipe. Plus it is really, really good. This makes a very good, healthful snack for everyone!—GMB*

**1.** Preheat the oven to 350°F.

**2.** Using a fork, mix together the first six ingredients.

**3.** Mix in the raisins and pecans. Let the mixture sit for 15 minutes.

**4.** Drop the batter onto a baking sheet by the spoonful. Bake 10 to 12 minutes.

**GMB Tip:** *To make this wheat-free, substitute 1 tablespoon of sorghum, cornmeal, oat flour, or ground pecan meal for the whole wheat flour.*

# GRANOLA BARS

¼ cup ground flax

¼ cup water

2 cups quick-cooking rolled oats

¼ cup whole grain spelt flour

1¾ cups total of chopped dried apples, cranberries, cherries (or another dried fruit), or chocolate chips.

½ cup chopped almonds

Pinch of sea salt

¼ cup extra virgin olive oil

¾ cup brown rice syrup

## Carol Anne Wasserman

**DAIRY-FREE**

Makes 36 bars

*These granola bars are so scrumptious, they make store-bought granola bars taste like cardboard. They are chock-full of good-for-you things and are easy to make. Because the only sweetener is brown rice syrup, they are also good for people with blood sugar issues.—GMB*

**1.** Preheat the oven to 350°F.

**2.** In a small mixing bowl, combine the ground flax and water to form a paste. Set aside.

**3.** In a separate bowl, thoroughly mix together the dry ingredients.

**4.** In a third bowl, mix together the olive oil and brown rice syrup. Add the flax paste.

**5.** Add the wet mixture to the dry ingredients and incorporate well.

**6.** Pour the batter into an 11×7½-inch baking pan, pressing the mixture down firmly. Bake for about 25 minutes, or until edges turn golden brown.

**7.** Let rest about 10 minutes until slightly cool, then cut.

**GMB Tip:** *To make these wheat-free, use ¼ cup oat flour instead of the spelt flour. You can do this by grinding oats in a blender or food processor until they are a fine meal. Just be sure to use oats that have not been contaminated with gluten.*

# OATMEAL RAISIN COOKIES

½ cup chopped walnuts (or pecans)

¾ cup (1½ sticks) butter, divided, at room temperature

1 cup maple sugar, finely ground

½ cup honey (or maple syrup)

1 large egg yolk, at room temperature

½ teaspoon vanilla extract

½ cup whole wheat pastry flour

¼ cup all-purpose flour

¼ teaspoon salt

¼ teaspoon baking powder

¼ teaspoon nutmeg

1½ cups rolled oats

1 cup raisins

¼ cup coconut (optional)

**GMB Tip:** *The maple syrup makes these cookies glisten, so they may look like they're not done when they really are. When they begin to brown around the edges, the air bubbles on top begin to break, and they spring back when gently poked with your finger—they're done!*

Makes 2 dozen cookies

*There's nothing better on a crisp fall morning than an oatmeal raisin cookie hot from the oven. This is a great basic cookie recipe that you can alter according to your tastes and what you have on hand. Add more nuts or grain-sweetened chocolate chips, coconut, or different dried fruits; it's hard to go wrong.—GMB*

**1.** Preheat the oven to 350°F.

**2.** Toast the nuts at 350°F for about 6 to 8 minutes, then mix with 1 tablespoon of butter while they are still hot. Set aside.

**3.** Place the remaining butter in a mixing bowl. Grind the maple sugar in a coffee or spice grinder. Add the maple sugar to the butter, mixing well and scraping down the sides of the bowl when necessary.

**4.** Gradually add the honey (or maple syrup) and mix until the batter is light and fluffy.

**5.** Add the egg yolk and vanilla extract. Beat until well blended.

**6.** Mix the flours with the salt, baking powder, nutmeg, and oats. Gradually add the dry ingredients to the wet mixture.

**7.** Fold in the raisins, buttered walnuts (or pecans), and coconut (if using).

**8.** Drop the batter by large spoonfuls onto baking sheets covered with parchment paper.

**9.** Bake the cookies for 10 to 12 minutes, or until they begin to brown. Don't overbake.

**10.** Remove the cookies from the oven. Leave them on the baking sheets for 1 minute, then cool on wire racks.

# NICK'S FAVORITE APPLE PIE

1 recipe Nick's Piecrust (see opposite or use Ann Harman's Foolproof Piecrust on page 127)

8 medium to large apples, cut into ½- to ¾-inch pieces

⅓ to ½ cup maple syrup (depending on sweetness of apples)

Cinnamon, nutmeg, and allspice to taste

1 tablespoon instant tapioca (or arrowroot)

**Nick Cowles**

Makes one 9-inch pie

*This tastes like an old-fashioned apple pie, but without the sugar! The maple syrup lends a rich sweetness that perfectly complements the fresh apples. You can easily substitute frozen apples (which you've put up yourself, of course) for the fresh apples when they're not in season.—GMB*

**1.** Preheat the oven to 350°F.

**2.** In a large skillet combine the apples, syrup, spices, and tapioca (or arrowroot). Simmer until the apples have softened. Let cool.

**3.** Take out the two piecrust balls from the refrigerator. Roll out one of the balls, using plenty of extra flour on the rolling pin, dough, and work surface. When the size is right (a 10-inch circle for a 9-inch pie), brush off the extra flour and set the dough in the pie plate. Repeat with the remaining dough, setting it aside in the refrigerator until you need it.

**4.** Pour the cooled apple mixture on top of the unbaked piecrust. Use water to slightly moisten the top edge of the bottom crust. Take the remaining crust out of the refrigerator and place it on top of the bottom crust. Crimp the edges. Slice two holes in the top of the crust to allow air to escape.

**5.** Bake for 35 to 40 minutes. (Check for doneness by poking a fork through one of the holes in the crust into an apple piece to see if it is soft.) Serve warm, at room temperature, or chilled.

# NICK'S PIECRUST

2 cups all-purpose flour

¾ cup (1½ sticks) cold butter, cut into ¼-inch pieces

⅓ cup ice-cold water

Pinch of salt

Makes two 9-inch crusts

**1.** In the bowl of a food processor, blend all the ingredients for less than 1 minute, or until the mixture clumps together. Divide the dough into two balls. Cover and chill in the refrigerator until needed.

**Nick's Special Crust Treatment:** *Soften 3 tablespoons of butter. Mix with 1 egg white. Brush the mixture all over the top crust (including the ruffled edge) after 15 to 20 minutes of cooking. Put the pie back into the oven. When the pie is done, the crust will be slightly golden brown and the filling will bubble and ooze a little. Let cool before slicing.*

# CRUNCHY OATMEAL WALNUT PIE

¼ recipe Foolproof Piecrust
(opposite, or use Nick's
Piecrust on page 125)

¼ cup butter

1⅓ cups honey

½ teaspoon cinnamon

¼ teaspoon cloves

¼ teaspoon salt

3 eggs

1 cup uncooked oatmeal

½ cup chopped nuts
(optional)

**Ann Harman**

Makes one 9-inch or 10-inch pie

*This pie is similar to a pecan pie, but with a layer of crispy-chewy oatmeal and nuts on top. It is moist and fabulous—wonderfully rich and gooey, though not over-the-top sweet.—GMB*

**1.** Prepare the piecrust by rolling out one of the dough patties, using plenty of flour on the rolling pin, dough, and work surface. When the size is right (a 10-inch circle for a 9-inch pie or an 11-inch circle for a 10-inch pie), brush off the extra flour and set the dough in the pie plate. Place it in the refrigerator until needed.

**2.** Preheat the oven to 350°F.

**3.** Cream the butter. Continue beating while adding the honey in a thin stream.

**4.** Add the cinnamon, cloves, and salt. Add the eggs one at a time, beating well after each addition. Stir in the oatmeal.

**5.** Pour the filling into the unbaked pie shell. Sprinkle the nuts (if using) on top of the pie. Bake for 50 minutes or until the pie is set.

# FOOLPROOF PIECRUST

4 cups all-purpose flour

2 teaspoons salt

1¾ cups butter

½ cup water

1 tablespoon white or cider vinegar

1 tablespoon honey

1 egg

Makes four 9½-inch or 10-inch crusts

*Here is a recipe for a foolproof piecrust (you can't destroy it!) that can be kept in the freezer for several months. When baking, protect the dough by covering the crust(s) loosely with foil. Note that it is a large recipe and makes four crusts.—Ann*

**1.** Mix the flour, salt, and butter with a fork until the dough is crumbly.

**2.** In a separate small bowl, beat together the water, vinegar, honey, and egg. Add it to the flour mixture, stirring until all the ingredients are moistened.

**3.** Divide the dough into four portions. Shape each piece of dough into a patty, wrap in plastic wrap, and chill for at least 30 minutes. This dough will keep up to 3 days in the refrigerator, or it can be frozen.

# BEAUTIFUL BROWN RICE PUDDING

1 cup almonds, skins removed

3 tablespoons tahini

2 cups water, divided

4 cups cooked long-grain brown rice

4 cups apple juice

½ cup raisins, optional

3 tablespoons rice syrup

1 cup strawberries

## Melanie Waxman

**DAIRY-FREE** **WHEAT-FREE** **LOW-FAT**

Serves 6 to 8

*This dessert is sweet enough to be completely satisfying, and healthful enough for you not to feel guilty.—GMB*

**1.** Preheat the oven to 350°F.

**2.** Put the almonds, tahini, and 1 cup of the water in a blender and mix well.

**3.** In a saucepan, combine the cooked rice, juice, raisins, and almond mixture. Cover and bring to a boil over medium heat.

**4.** Reduce the heat and simmer for about 10 minutes. Add the remaining cup of water and mix. The mixture should be quite watery.

**5.** Place the rice mixture in a baking dish and cover with a lid. Bake for 20 minutes. Remove the lid during the last 5 minutes of baking to brown the top.

**6.** Blend the rice syrup and strawberries in the blender. Serve on top of the rice pudding.

**GMB Tip:** *For variety, add 1 teaspoon vanilla extract or 1 teaspoon lemon rind to the almond mixture.*

# PECAN PIE

1 9-inch piecrust (see Foolproof Piecrust on page 127 or Nick's Piecrust on page 125)
3 eggs
½ cup maple syrup
⅓ cup brown rice syrup
1 teaspoon vanilla extract
1 pinch salt
1¼ cups pecan pieces
3 tablespoons butter

Makes one 9-inch pie

*As Georgia natives, we had to include a pecan pie recipe! This is one of our favorite holiday pies. Serve with a dollop of maple-sweetened whipped cream or, for an amazingly decadent dessert, serve with a scoop of Maple Ice Cream (see page 149).—GMB*

**1.** Preheat the oven to 350°F.

**2.** In a mixing bowl, beat the eggs until frothy, then add the maple syrup and brown rice syrup.

**3.** Add the vanilla extract and salt.

**4.** Sauté the pecan pieces in butter in a large frying pan for 3 to 4 minutes, then allow to cool.

**5.** Add the cooled pecan mixture to the egg mixture and stir until all ingredients are well blended.

**6.** Pour into an unbaked pie shell. Bake for 25 to 30 minutes, or until set.

**7.** Serve with sweetened whipped cream.

# PUMPKIN PIE AND CUSTARD

1 9-inch piecrust, if making pie (see page 125 or 127)

1 cup brown rice syrup, barley malt syrup, or maple syrup

½ teaspoon salt

1½ teaspoons cinnamon

½ teaspoon powdered ginger (or 4 tablespoons finely grated fresh ginger)

½ teaspoon cloves

1½ cups cooked or canned pumpkin, mashed or puréed

1½ cups cream*

½ cup milk*

2 eggs, slightly beaten

* Adjust proportion of milk and cream to suit your tastes. Use 2 cups total of milk and cream combined.

## Debra Lynn Dadd

Makes one 9-inch pie or 4 to 5 ramekins of custard

You can use (organic) canned pumpkin, though fresh is better. Cookbooks recommend steaming pumpkin, but I roast it to concentrate the flavor. Place a halved and cleaned pumpkin in a roasting pan or on a cookie sheet and roast at 350°F for about 25 to 30 minutes, or until the flesh is soft. Wash the seeds, spread them on a cookie sheet, and roast them in the oven along with the pumpkin, for about 10 minutes. We like to put butter and salt on them. They are best hot out of the oven.—Debra Lynn

1. Preheat the oven to 425°F.

2. Combine all the ingredients in a large bowl and beat with an electric mixer until the mixture is smooth.

3. To make custards, pour the mixture into individual custard cups or ramekins. To make a pie, pour the mixture into a 9-inch unbaked pie shell.

4. Bake for 10 minutes, then lower the heat to 300°F and bake for another 45 minutes, or until the filling is firm. Ramekins will be done sooner, in about 30 minutes.

*Debra Lynn was generous enough to share some of her research with us. She is untiring in her efforts to combine good taste and good health. You might want to try some of her other natural sweetener suggestions. We used maple syrup. YUM!—GMB*

Debra Lynn tested this recipe with eight different sweeteners. This is what she had to say: "My husband and I tasted them all. This really showed the difference between sweeteners and reinforced for me that different sweeteners are best suited for different uses. Here are a few of the results."

**RICE SYRUP AND BARLEY MALT SYRUP** I tried these separately, then combined half and half. Barley malt alone was too strong and very dark. Rice syrup alone was very light and not very sweet. The combination of the two was perfect. The molasses taste of the barley malt gave the rice syrup a nice depth of flavor.

**MAPLE SYRUP** We both liked this for sweetness. It didn't have a very strong maple flavor, but there was a little maple aftertaste. I like the idea of using maple syrup with pumpkin because they are both so quintessentially American. If you really want maple flavor in your pumpkin, use Grade B maple syrup, which is stronger, or add a little maple flavor extract.

# HONEY-FIGGY TOFFEE PUDDING

## PUDDING

7 ounces dried figs

½ cup bourbon

½ cup warm water

7 tablespoons butter, softened, plus more for coating 12 ramekins

1½ cups all-purpose flour

1½ teaspoons baking powder

⅛ teaspoon baking soda

½ teaspoon kosher salt

½ teaspoon ground cinnamon

¼ teaspoon freshly ground nutmeg

¼ teaspoon ground ginger

¾ cup Tupelo honey (or other full-bodied honey)

2 large eggs

1 recipe Toffee Sauce (see step 9 on opposite page)

Softly whipped cream or crème fraîche

## TOFFEE SAUCE

1¾ cups heavy cream

1 cup Tupelo honey

1 cup maple syrup

8 tablespoons unsalted butter

⅓ cup bourbon

2½ teaspoons kosher salt

### Cynthia Wong

Serves 12

*When we bit into this incredibly rich and decadent figgy pudding at the Cakes and Ales restaurant in Decatur, Georgia, where Cynthia Wong is the pastry chef, we knew we had to include the recipe in this book. The combination of honey, figs, bourbon, and maple syrup makes this a truly fabulous dessert.—GMB*

**1.** Preheat the oven to 350°F.

**2.** Chop the dried figs into small pieces. Place them in a small saucepan with the bourbon and water. Bring to a boil over medium heat, then lower the heat, cover, and simmer for 8 to 10 minutes, or until most of the liquid has been absorbed and the figs are soft.

**3.** Transfer the figs and any remaining liquid into the bowl of a food processor. Process the figs until they form a smooth purée. Set aside to cool slightly.

**4.** Generously butter 12 wide-mouth, half-pint canning jars or ramekins. Set them aside.

**5.** Sift together the flour, baking powder, baking soda, salt, cinnamon, nutmeg, and ginger. Set aside.

**6.** Place the butter in the bowl of an electric stand mixer. Using the paddle attachment, mix the butter on low speed until it is creamy. Add the honey and continue beating on low speed until the mixture is combined, then increase the speed to medium and cream until light and fluffy. Add the eggs, one at a time, and continue beating on medium speed, scraping down the sides of the bowl as necessary.

**7.** Add half the flour mixture to the mixing bowl, beating on low speed. Increase the speed to medium and mix until just combined. Add all the fig purée and mix on low speed until just combined. Mix in the remaining flour mixture on low speed, increasing to medium speed until the batter is just combined.

**8.** Divide the batter evenly between jars or ramekins. Set them on a rimmed cookie sheet and place in the middle rack of the oven.

**9.** Bake for 25 minutes, rotating halfway through the cooking time. The cakes should be golden brown on the top and sides, and a toothpick inserted into the center should come out clean. While the cakes are baking, make the Toffee Sauce by placing all the ingredients in a small saucepan, bringing it to a boil over medium heat, then lowering the heat and simmering for 5 minutes, until mixture is the thickness of maple syrup.

**10.** When the cakes are done, poke them all over with a skewer or paring knife. While they are still hot, pour the Toffee Sauce over them. Save any leftover sauce to serve on the side.

**11.** Once the jars are cool enough to handle, screw on the lids. The puddings will keep for 3 days at room temperature and a week in the refrigerator. To reheat the pudding, remove the lid and place it in a preheated 350°F oven for 8 to 10 minutes, or until the sauce has melted and is bubbly.

**GMB Tip:** *The puddings can be served in jars or ramekins or turned out onto dessert plates. Very carefully run a small knife between the pudding and the container, pressing the blade against the container. Place the plate on top of the jar, then invert it. Serve with whipped cream or whipped crème fraîche.*

# APPLESAUCE WALNUT BREAD

2 teaspoons dry yeast

1 cup warm water

1 cup Applesauce (see page 148)

3 tablespoons oil

1 cup cold buttermilk

4 to 5½ cups whole wheat bread flour

2½ teaspoons salt

⅔ cup chopped walnuts, toasted

**GMB Tip:** *If you don't have whole wheat bread flour, use 1½ cups white unbleached bread flour and 3 to 4 cups whole wheat flour.*

**Ronit Gourarie**

Makes 2 loaves

*Since this is a great gift-giving bread, you can make it fancier by baking it hearth-style in a pie tin, or by putting a shine on the crust (either with an egg wash or by brushing it with butter after the loaf comes out of the oven), or by using the dough to make round dinner rolls in a baking pan or muffin tins.*

*When giving bread as a gift, put the freshly baked bread into a paper bag, as a plastic bag will create condensation, resulting in a soggy crust. Consider keeping decorative paper bags on hand for this purpose.—Ronit*

**1.** Dissolve the yeast in the warm water.

**2.** Heat the applesauce, then slowly stir in the oil and cold buttermilk. Add to the yeast mixture.

**3.** Measure 4½ cups of whole wheat bread flour into a large glass or ceramic mixing bowl. Make a well in the center of the flour and pour the liquid ingredients into it. Stir from the center outward to form a smooth batter, then fold and stir the remaining flour, as needed, into the liquid.

**4.** Turn the dough out onto a table and knead it for 8 to 10 minutes, or until elastic. After about 5 minutes of kneading, add the salt. Toward the end of the kneading time, knead in the walnuts until they are well distributed. Form the dough into a ball and place it back in the mixing bowl.

**5.** Cover the dough and place it in a warm, draft-free place to rise. It will take between 1½ and 2 hours to rise fully; test it by making a half-inch hole in the dough with your wet fingertip; if the hole fills in slightly, give the dough a bit more time; if the hole remains and the dough sighs, deflate and let rise again, which will take about an hour.

**6.** Divide the dough in half and shape it into loaves by rolling each half into a rectangle the length of the loaf pan you are using. Tightly roll the rectangle, placing the seam down in a greased loaf pan, and let the dough rise for 45 to 60 minutes prior to baking.

**7.** Bake at 350°F for 45 to 60 minutes (high-rising loaves take the least time). Let the bread sit before slicing it.

# BLACK GRAPE SWEET BREAD

1 tablespoon yeast
(1½ packages)

½ cup warm water

⅓ cup plus 2 tablespoons
honey, divided

2 to 2½ cups bread flour (or
all-purpose flour)

½ teaspoon salt

⅓ cup extra virgin olive oil

2 cups seeded black grapes,
cut in half lengthwise
(you can substitute green
grapes if you can't find
black)

Serves 20 to 24

*My husband and I first had this delicious bread when visiting Tuscany.
I was determined to figure out how to make it, and this recipe is pretty
close! The dough is slightly sweetened with honey, but the real sweetness
comes from the grapes. It makes me wonder why we don't bake with
grapes more often. They are sweet, juicy, and delicious! —GMB*

**1.** Mix the yeast and 1 tablespoon of the honey in the warm
water and let it sit for 10 to 15 minutes, or until frothy.

**2.** Sift 1½ cups of the flour and the salt into a large mixing
bowl, then make a well in the center.

**3.** Add the olive oil and ⅓ cup honey (reserving the
remaining 2 tablespoons for later) to the yeast and pour the
mixture into the flour. Gradually mix together, adding more
flour as needed until the dough sticks together and can be
handled.

**4.** Knead the dough for about 5 to 10 minutes.

**5.** Let the dough rise 1 hour or until almost doubled.

**6.** Punch down the dough, shape it into a ball, cover it, then
allow it to rise again for about 45 to 60 minutes.

**7.** Grease a 9×13-inch baking pan.

**8.** Divide the dough in half. Press one piece in the pan and
gently stretch it until the dough covers the bottom. Press
1 cup of cut grapes into the dough. Drizzle 1 tablespoon of
warm honey on top.

**9.** Roll out the second half of the dough and use it to cover
the first piece. Press the remaining grapes into the top
dough and drizzle with the remaining honey.

**10.** Allow the dough to rise one more time, for about an
hour. While the dough rises, preheat the oven to 375°F.

**11.** Bake for 30 minutes.

# BRANDIED PUMPKIN GINGERBREAD

1 cup pumpkin, cooked and puréed

⅓ cup oil (sunflower or canola)

2 eggs

¾ cup honey

1 cup unbleached all-purpose white flour

¾ cup whole wheat flour

1 teaspoon baking soda

¼ teaspoon salt

½ teaspoon cinnamon

¼ teaspoon fresh nutmeg, grated

3 tablespoons apricot brandy (or apricot nectar)

¾ cup dried cranberries*

2 tablespoons freshly grated ginger**

½ cup chopped walnuts

\* *original recipe called for ½ cup dried cranberries*

\*\* *original recipe called for ¼ cup candied ginger*

**Kathy Schlosser**
Makes 1 standard loaf

*A display of small heirloom pumpkins at a local farmers' market inspired me to try something a little different with their flavorful orange flesh. This recipe combines the best of gingerbread and pumpkin bread in a moist sweet bread with a little flair. If you prepare the pumpkin ahead of time, storing it in measured containers in the freezer, you can make the bread quickly, filling the house with a tantalizing fragrance of fall.—Kathy*

**1.** Preheat the oven to 350°F. (Reduce heat to 325°F if using glass pans.)

**2.** In a large bowl, blend the pumpkin, oil, eggs, and honey.

**3.** In a separate bowl, stir together the flours, baking soda, salt, cinnamon, and nutmeg.

**4.** Gradually add the flour mixture to the pumpkin mixture, alternating with the brandy. Blend thoroughly. Stir in the cranberries, ginger, and nuts.

**5.** Pour the mixture into a greased-and-floured loaf pan (approximately 4½×8 inches), or two slightly smaller pans. Bake for 45 minutes, or until a toothpick inserted into the center of the bread comes out clean. Allow to sit in pan for 10 minutes, then remove and place onto rack to finish cooling.

# FIG AND BASIL MUFFINS

1½ cups unbleached all-purpose flour

1 cup stone-ground yellow cornmeal

½ teaspoon salt

2 teaspoons baking powder

1 cup chopped figs

1 extra-large egg

1⅓ cups milk

¼ cup olive oil

¼ cup mild-flavored honey

1 cup basil leaves, coarsely chopped

**Susan Belsinger**

from *Basil: An Herb Lover's Guide* (Interweave, 1996)

Makes 12 muffins

*These golden, toothsome little muffins are full of unusual flavors—the honey and figs provide sweetness, the basil lends a lovely perfume, and the olive oil and cornmeal give them a delicious wholesome taste. Use whatever type of fig you prefer; Black Mission figs are my favorite. If the figs are very dry, soak them in warm water for 15 minutes or so, then pat them dry. As for basils, Genovese, Aussie Sweetie (also known as Lesbos or Green Column), Spicy Globe, or even Cinnamon (named for its distinct cinnamon aroma) are good choices. These muffins are best served warm. To reheat, wrap them in foil and heat them at 300°F for about 15 minutes.—Susan*

**1.** Preheat the oven to 400°F. Prepare the muffin pan with paper liners or by generously buttering it.

**2.** Mix the flour, cornmeal, salt, and baking powder in a bowl. Toss in the figs. Make a well in the dry ingredients.

**3.** In a separate bowl, lightly beat the egg. Add the milk, oil, and honey and blend well. Stir in the basil. Pour the liquid ingredients into the dry ingredients and stir until just mixed.

**4.** Fill the muffin cups with the batter, almost to the rim. Bake for 20 to 22 minutes, until the muffins are golden brown. Allow the muffins to cool for several minutes before serving.

# PUMPKIN RAISIN MUFFINS

⅓ cup plus 3 tablespoons hot water

1½ cups raisins

3 large eggs at room temperature

¾ cup honey

1 cup malt barley syrup and maple syrup combined

1 15-ounce can (1½ cups) pumpkin purée

1½ teaspoons vanilla extract

1 cup plus 2 tablespoons light olive oil

1½ cups unbleached all-purpose flour

1 cup whole wheat flour

2¼ teaspoons cinnamon

2¼ teaspoons ground cloves

2¼ teaspoons baking powder

2¼ teaspoons baking soda

1 teaspoon salt

Makes 20–24 muffins

*This was one of the first recipes we tried using natural sweeteners and it is still a favorite. This is a great muffin to serve when the weather turns cool in the fall. You can also make these as mini muffins, making them great after-school treats.—GMB*

**1.** Preheat the oven to 350°F. Prepare the muffin pans either with a coating of butter or by using paper liners.

**2.** Pour the hot water over the raisins and let them sit.

**3.** Beat the eggs until they are lemon yellow in color. Add the honey and syrups until the mixture thickens slightly. Blend in the pumpkin and vanilla extract.

**4.** Pour in the oil and continue mixing, scraping down the bowl to thoroughly blend. Drain the water off the raisins and add them to the batter.

**5.** In a separate bowl, mix together the flours, spices, baking powder, baking soda, and salt. Add the dry ingredients to the pumpkin mixture and combine until just blended.

**6.** Fill the muffin cups almost full. Bake for 20 minutes, or until a toothpick inserted into the center comes out clean. (Mini muffins will take about 15 minutes.)

**7.** Cool the muffins on a wire rack. Store at room temperature in an airtight container or freeze for several months until needed.

# SORGHUM GINGERBREAD

1 cup sorghum

½ cup honey*

1 cup butter

2 eggs, beaten

½ teaspoon salt

2½ cups flour

1½ teaspoons baking soda

1 teaspoon ginger

1 teaspoon cinnamon

¾ cup hot water**

\* *original recipe called for ½ cup sugar*

\*\* *original recipe called for 1 cup hot water*

**National Sweet Sorghum Producers and Processors Association**

Makes one 9×12-inch pan

*This is a really nice, moist gingerbread, perfect to serve with homemade Applesauce (see recipe page 148). The sorghum adds a delicious and unique flavor.—GMB*

**1.** Preheat the oven to 350°F.

**2.** In a mixing bowl, cream the sorghum, honey, and butter. Add the eggs, and mix well.

**3.** Add the dry ingredients to the wet mixture and stir until well blended.

**4.** Add the hot water and stir until well mixed. Do not overmix.

**5.** Pour into a 9×12-inch prepared pan, and bake for 35 minutes, or until a toothpick inserted into the center comes out clean.

# SWEET POTATO BREAD

3½ cups all-purpose flour
1 teaspoon salt
2 teaspoons baking soda
¼ teaspoon cinnamon
½ teaspoon nutmeg
2 teaspoons orange peel
3 eggs
½ cup vegetable oil
2 cups sweet potato purée
1 teaspoon vanilla extract
1½ cups maple syrup

**Sonya Jones**
Makes 1 standard loaf

*Sweet potatoes are one of Sonya's specialties. "They're so overlooked for baking!" she told us. This bread is proof that sweet potatoes make an excellent base for sweet breads, muffins, pies, cakes, and cookies.*
*—GMB*

**1.** Preheat the oven to 350°F.

**2.** In a mixing bowl, combine the dry ingredients, including the orange peel.

**3.** In a separate bowl, mix the wet ingredients. Make a well in the center of the dry mixture and add the wet ingredients, stirring until just blended.

**4.** Pour the batter into a lightly greased and floured 8½×4½×3-inch loaf pan.

**5.** Bake for 45 to 55 minutes or until a toothpick inserted in the center comes out clean. Cool the bread in the pan for 10 minutes.

**6.** Remove the bread from the pan by inverting the pan onto a serving plate. This is delicious served warm or cold!

**GMB Tip:** *For a slightly different texture and extra color, add ¾ cup cranberries to the batter after the wet and dry ingredients are combined.*

# PERSIMMON BREAD

2 cups all-purpose flour
(or 1 cup all-purpose flour
and 1 cup whole wheat
flour)

½ teaspoon baking soda

½ teaspoon salt

2 teaspoons baking powder

1 teaspoon cinnamon

½ teaspoon nutmeg

1 cup persimmon pulp

½ cup milk

½ cup maple syrup*

⅓ cup brown rice syrup*

2 eggs

¼ cup (½ stick) butter

1 cup chopped walnuts
(optional)

* *original recipe called for
1 cup sugar instead of the
maple and rice syrups*

**Charles Sanders**

Makes 1 loaf

*Persimmons offer a wonderful and unusual taste in this bread. Wild persimmons are best, of course, but commercially available ones will do the trick as well. The bread is slightly sweet and is nice with a cup of tea or coffee.—GMB*

**1.** Preheat the oven to 350°F.

**2.** Sift together the dry ingredients.

**3.** In a separate bowl, mix together the persimmon pulp, milk, syrups, and eggs. Grate butter into the mixture.

**4.** Add the dry ingredients to the wet ingredients and mix until well blended. Stir in the chopped nuts (if using).

**5.** Pour the batter into a well-greased 9×5×3-inch loaf pan and bake for 45 minutes.

**6.** Cool on racks before slicing.

# ROSEMARY BUTTERMILK BISCUITS

3 cups all-purpose flour

1 cup whole wheat pastry flour

1½ tablespoons minced fresh rosemary

4¼ teaspoons baking powder

1 teaspoon baking soda

1½ teaspoons salt

¾ cup (1½ sticks) Organic Valley European-style cultured butter (or any high-fat, high-quality butter), frozen*

2 cups Organic Valley cultured low-fat buttermilk

\* *European style butters have a higher fat content, resulting in flakier baked goods.*

**Terese Allen, of Organic Valley**
Makes 12 to 13 biscuits

*There's nothing like biscuits right out of the oven, but producing them can be tricky when you're in the last-minute throes of meal preparation. To make it easier, prepare the flour-butter mixture and measure out the buttermilk ahead of time, then keep them both refrigerated. Reserve a corner of your counter for biscuit assembly: flour the work surface and near it arrange a rolling pin, baking pan, and cloth-lined basket for serving the biscuits. Then, about 15 minutes before serving time, add the buttermilk to the biscuit dough, cut out the biscuits, and bake them.—Terese*

**1.** Preheat the oven to 425°F.

**2.** In a large bowl, thoroughly whisk together the flours, rosemary, baking powder, baking soda, and salt. Using the large holes of a handheld grater, grate the frozen butter directly into the flour mixture. Combine.

**3.** Make a well in the center of the flour mixture, pour in the buttermilk, and use a fork to stir until the mixture just barely forms a dough.

**4.** Transfer to a lightly floured surface and gently but briefly knead it 4 or 5 turns. Using a floured rolling pin or your fingers, roll or lightly press the dough out to ¾ inch thick. Use a floured 3-inch biscuit cutter to cut out rounds, taking care to slice straight down into the dough without twisting the cutter. (This will help the biscuits rise.) Gather any dough scraps, press them together, and cut additional biscuits.

**5.** Transfer the biscuits to an ungreased baking pan (an inch or two apart for crusty exteriors, or close together for soft-sided biscuits). Bake for 10 to 13 minutes, or until golden brown. Serve hot or warm.

# MESQUITE CORNBREAD

¾ cup cornmeal

¾ cup all-purpose flour

⅓ cup mesquite meal

2 teaspoons baking powder

½ teaspoon baking soda

½ teaspoon salt

1 cup yogurt

1 egg

3 tablespoons agave nectar or honey

3 tablespoons oil

**Beverly Cox**
from *Native Peoples* magazine
Makes one 8×8-inch pan

*We loved this slightly sweet cornbread. The mesquite meal (made from grinding the beans of the mesquite tree) offers a flavor that hints at chocolate. It is truly an unusual and delightful cornbread.—GMB*

**1.** Preheat the oven to 350°F.

**2.** In a medium bowl, combine the dry ingredients together.

**3.** In a separate bowl, combine the wet ingredients. Stir the wet mixture into the dry ingredients until just combined.

**4.** Spread into a greased 8×8-inch pan. Bake 20 to 25 minutes.

**GMB Tip:** *For a unique Southwestern kick, add 1 tablespoon chipotle (dried, smoked jalapeño) flakes and ¾ cup fresh or frozen corn kernels.*

# DILL RICOTTA TORTE

1 cup almonds

1½ cups whole wheat bread crumbs

½ cup unsalted butter, softened

¼ teaspoon salt

¾ pound (12 ounces) natural cream cheese, softened

1 cup ricotta cheese

2 eggs

2 tablespoons half-and-half

⅓ cup fresh dill leaves

½ teaspoon freshly grated nutmeg

1 teaspoon grated lemon peel

Dill sprigs for garnish

**Susan Belsinger**
from *Herbs in the Kitchen* (Interweave, 1991)
Serves 8 to 12

*We like serving this savory, rich torte for Sunday brunch or lunch as a change from the more usual egg and cheese dishes. The torte can be baked ahead of time, cooled to room temperature, then refrigerated for a day or so. It goes well with a variety of fruit and green salads and a selection of sliced ham or smoked fish. Natural cream cheese, without gums or chemicals, is available in many markets, cheese stores, and delicatessens; in our opinion, it has a finer flavor than processed cream cheese.—Susan*

**1.** Preheat the oven to 350°F.

**2.** Make a medium-fine almond meal using a blender or food processor. Transfer the almond meal to a bowl and combine it with the bread crumbs.

**3.** Mix the softened butter with the almond meal, bread crumbs, and salt, blending well. Press the mixture on the bottom and sides of a 9½-inch springform pan.

**4.** With an electric mixer on medium speed, or with a food processor, combine the cheeses, eggs, half-and-half, dill leaves, nutmeg, and grated lemon peel. Blend the mixture very well and season with additional salt to taste.

**5.** Pour the mixture carefully into the springform pan and bake for 1 hour and 10 minutes. Cool to room temperature on a rack. Remove springform ring and garnish torte with dill sprigs. May also be served chilled.

# RUSTIC GRILLED PIZZA

1 package active dry yeast

1 tablespoon honey
(optional)

1⅔ cups warm water (105
to 115°F)

1¾ cups unbleached all-
purpose flour

1 cup whole wheat flour

1 cup spelt flour

Heaping tablespoon
of sea salt

2 tablespoons olive oil

Chopped rosemary,
parsley, or oregano
(optional)

Cornmeal
for pizza stone

Sauce, cheese, other
toppings

Makes three 12×15-inch pizzas

*This is a great recipe for a gathering of family and friends. Everyone can get in on the act—rolling out the dough or adding the toppings. It's a good way to involve a lot of people and to use a lot of fresh produce. Our pizza ingredients change with the seasons, but they all seem to be delicious! You will need a pizza baking stone for this recipe.—GMB*

**1.** Light coals or preheat the oven to 425°F. (Plan on preheating the pizza stone for at least 30 minutes before rolling out the crusts and making the pizzas.)

**2.** Dissolve the yeast and honey (if using) in the warm water and let it stand for 5 minutes, or until bubbly.

**3.** In a large bowl, mix the flours and salt. In a small bowl, whisk together the oil and the yeast mixture.

**4.** Pour the liquid mixture into the dry ingredients and mix with a wooden spoon until a dough forms. Add the fresh herbs (if using) to the dough before starting to mix. If the dough is too stiff, add more room-temperature water, a little at a time. If the dough is too wet, add more flour. Once the dough is formed, knead for 10 minutes on a lightly floured tabletop.

**5.** Place the dough in a bowl (lightly coated with oil) and cover for about 1 to 1½ hours, or until doubled in size.

**6.** Cut the dough into 3 separate pieces. Punch down each piece and roll it into a ball.

**7.** Cover the dough balls and let them rest for about 15 minutes, or a little longer. Dough should be elastic and easy to roll out, as opposed to springing back.

**8.** Roll out one ball of dough to the desired thickness, about the same size and shape as the pizza stone. Keep the other balls of dough covered until they are ready to use, or freeze for later use.

**9.** Sprinkle cornmeal on the preheated stone to prevent the dough from sticking.

**10.** Place the rolled dough on the pizza stone. Grill or bake for about 8 minutes, or until the bottom of the crust begins to brown.

**11.** Move the crust from the stone onto a clean surface, brushing off excess cornmeal.

**12.** Put sauce, cheese, and desired toppings on the unbaked side of the crust. For toppings, use whatever is in season at your local market. **Note:** *In the fall, we like to use arugula or Swiss chard; homemade pepperoni or sausage; local cheeses such as Brie, fresh mozzarella, or Guinness cheddar; pesto; wild mushrooms; and caramelized onions.*

**13.** Sprinkle the stone with more cornmeal if necessary, and place the prepared pizza on the stone. Grill another 8 to 10 minutes, until the cheese is melted.

**14.** Repeat with the other balls of dough. The pizza should be smoky and delicious.

# APPLESAUCE

7 medium to large apples, such as Granny Smith, peeled, cored, and cut into bite-size pieces

Apple juice (or water)

½ cup maple syrup or honey, if needed

1 teaspoon cinnamon

¼ teaspoon salt

Makes 3 pints

*During apple season, somebody in the house is always peeling, paring, saucing, or pie-ing—or just eating!—apples. The following is a basic recipe that can be changed to suit your tastes.—GMB*

**1.** Place the apples in a small saucepan and add enough juice or water to almost cover the apples. Cook over medium heat until the apple pieces are tender. Sweeten to taste with the maple syrup or honey.

**2.** Add the cinnamon and salt.

**3.** Purée in a blender or food processor if desired, or leave chunky.

**4.** If desired, put sauce in sterilized glass canning jars and process for about 10 minutes. (See instructions in "Preserving the Harvest," pages 185–190.)

**GMB Tip:** *You can make pear sauce this same way, though pears are usually sweet enough that you don't have to add much (if any) sweetener. It is absolutely delicious.*

# MAPLE ICE CREAM

1 cup maple syrup
1 cup heavy cream
2 cups whole milk
¼ teaspoon salt
2 large eggs

Makes 1 quart

*This is one of those oh-my-gosh recipes. It is very, very rich and amazingly delicious. It's mostly cream and maple syrup—how could you go wrong? Use it sparingly, as a little goes a long way. Of course, you can alter the richness by changing the cream and milk ratios. As long as you include a total of 3 cups of cream and/or milk, it should turn out fine. You can also use light cream. Add ⅓ cup toasted pecans or walnuts for a special treat.—GMB*

**1.** Boil the syrup in a saucepan for about 6 to 8 minutes, or until it has reduced to ¾ cup. **Note:** *The syrup gets extremely hot. Use a glass measuring cup rather than a plastic one to measure hot syrup.*

**2.** Stir in the cream, milk, and salt. Return the mixture to a boil.

**3.** Whisk the eggs in a large bowl, then gradually add the hot cream mixture in a stream, whisking continually.

**4.** Pour this mixture back into the saucepan and cook over medium-low heat for about 2 to 3 minutes, or until the mixture is thick and coats the back of a spoon. Do not boil.

**5.** Pour the syrup into a metal bowl and place it in a larger bowl full of ice. Whisk until the mixture has cooled. Cover with plastic wrap and chill in the fridge for several hours.

**6.** Freeze in an ice cream maker according to the manufacturer's directions.

Cheeses
Chocolate
Citrus fruits
Coconut
Cranberries
Dates
Dill
Dried fruits
Mushrooms
Nuts
Oats
Onions
Pomegranates
Raisins
Seeds
Spices

ALTHOUGH I TEND TO BELIEVE THAT *EVERY* SEASON IS BAKING SEASON, I like baking best in winter. I love the way everything seems to warm up from the heat of the kitchen, which is the heart of the home, and have to smile when the kids come into the house and say, "It smells so good in here—what's baking?"

Sometimes I think the end product is only part of the reason that I bake. After all, if it's only taste that I want, I can find someplace to buy baked goods, but if it's the whole experience—the feel of the dough, the magic as it rises, the smell as it bakes, the sense of home that it evokes—then I'm just going to have to do it myself. There's no other way to duplicate the experience.

During the weeks leading up to the holidays, the kitchen smells rich and spicy as I bake volumes of cakes, breads, muffins, and cookies to give away to friends and family. Fresh cranberries go into honey-sweetened cranberry sauce for holiday dinners, while handfuls of dried cranberries are put into the granola that I give away, each bag tied with a bright gingham ribbon.

The freezer door swings open and shut as often as the oven door, as I pull out bag after bag of treasures that I put away during the harvest months. Strawberries are transformed into glistening jams and jellies; raspberries, blackberries, and peaches are made into pies or muffins. Winter is the time to raid the freezer, pop open a row of home-canned goods, crack the nuts, chop the dates, and—maybe the best!—indulge in the dark, bitter chocolate you've been saving.

We have offered you some of the most perfectly delectable, naturally sweetened chocolate desserts you can imagine. Try a batch of Christina Pirello's great Chocolate Peanut Butter Cookies (page 165) or Alex Jamieson's Chocolate Tofu Pudding (page 170). When you grow tired of chocolate (if that's possible), make Annie Stilwell Burch's fabulous Lemon Raspberry Tart (page 172). It's wonderful and impressive.

As you sit in the kitchen waiting for your latest masterpiece to finish baking, pour a cup of tea and sit down for a few minutes. Savor the smells, enjoy the warmth of your home, jump up and take a peek at the treasures baking inside the oven, and know that there is absolutely nothing that can compare to the experience of baking. Enjoy!

· · · · · · ·

## Choosing Produce

CHOCOLATE Chocolate comes from the bean of the cocoa tree and appears in many forms, including unsweetened, bittersweet, and semisweet. Cocoa is produced by taking the cocoa butter out of chocolate, leaving a rich, bitter powder.

Different kinds of chocolates are determined by the quantity of pure chocolate liquor present. Unsweetened, bittersweet, semisweet, and milk chocolate all contain varying amounts of cocoa butter, chocolate liquor, and sugar and vanilla (except unsweetened chocolate, which doesn't have sugar, of course). White chocolate is not technically a "chocolate", since it contains only cocoa butter, milk solids, sugar, and vanilla, but no chocolate liquor.

One of the things that makes chocolate such a pleasure is that it is a solid at room temperature but melts at mouth temperature. You can store chocolate for a very long time (several years for dark, unsweetened chocolate) if you put it in a cool, dry place (but not in the refrigerator). The whitish substance that sometimes appears on chocolate is simply the cocoa butter that has separated out. It is completely harmless.

Grain-sweetened chocolate chips are a gift to bakers who avoid refined sugars. These little nuggets are sweetened with malted grains (barley and corn) and are fabulous for use wherever you would use traditional chocolate chips.

Be sure to melt chocolate at temperatures below 115°F. The favored method involves using a double boiler. When adding liquids such as maple syrup to chocolate, add the liquid before melting the chocolate to avoid ending up with a lumpy or grainy mixture. Using the microwave to melt chocolate is fine as long as you do it slowly, at a low temperature, and stop to stir it often (every 10 seconds or so).

CITRUS FRUITS Choose fruit that is firm and heavy. Don't buy citrus fruits that have soft or spongy spots or that look moldy. Store in the refrigerator for about two weeks, or at room temperature for a few days.

To get the greatest amount of juice, use room temperature fruit and roll it on the counter with the palm of your hand to help break down the pulp. Use freshly squeezed lemon or orange juice within a day or two, as it quickly loses flavor. You can pour the juice into small ice cube trays to freeze for later use. You can also freeze cut lemons (just don't try to freeze them whole).

*The amount of juice you get from a lemon depends on the lemon itself. Some are nice and juicy, but sometimes you . . . um . . . get a lemon. In general, though, you can count on the following:*

- 1 medium lemon: about ¼ cup of juice
- 3 medium lemons: ½ cup of juice
- 6 medium lemons: a little over 1 cup of juice

If you need only a few drops, poke holes in the lemon with a fork, squeeze out the few drops, and return it to the refrigerator.

One orange yields approximately ¼ cup of juice. The amount of juice from a lime varies from 1 to 2 tablespoons.

COCONUT Unfortunately, many of the "fresh" coconuts we buy have traveled a long way and are not actually very fresh. In the United States the coconut palm tree grows only in Hawaii and Florida, so unless you live in those states, it's hard to obtain local coconut.

To open a whole coconut, place a knife blade in one of the "eyes" and drain out the water (save this for cooking rice or for drinking), then double-bag the fruit (using plastic bags from the grocery store), and slam the coconut against a stone or concrete. The impact will break open the fruit and will usually separate the meat as well. If you don't have stone or concrete to slam the coconut against, an alternative method is to wrap the coconut in an old towel and use a hammer to smash the coconut open. Use a small knife to pry away the white meat from the shell. Once you've separated all the meat from the husk, grate it with a cheese grater or use a vegetable peeler to make coconut flakes or shavings. If you purchase the coconut already grated, make sure it is unsweetened. Stored in the refrigerator or freezer, it will last for months.

CRANBERRIES Testing cranberries to see if they're fresh is child's play, literally—you toss them onto a counter to see if they

bounce. This is rarely necessary (though a lot of fun) because fresh cranberries last for weeks in the refrigerator. This is a good thing since the harvest season is so short (September through November). Fortunately, cranberries are also easy to put up and can be frozen or dried to be enjoyed throughout the year. Freeze them on a cookie sheet, then pack them in plastic freezer bags.

DRIED FRUITS Store at room temperature or slightly cooler, in airtight containers. They should last up to a year if stored in a cool, dry place.

MUSHROOMS Mushrooms should be purchased as fresh as possible. Don't even bother buying them if they already look slick or shriveled—they will not improve with age. Choose firm, moist, fresh-looking mushrooms that aren't bruised or discolored. Store them in a brown paper bag in the refrigerator (plastic increases moisture and hastens disintegration).

You usually don't need to wash mushrooms. Simply wipe them clean with a damp rag. If you feel compelled to wash them, plunge them into cool water for a few seconds and drain immediately. Fresh mushrooms stay good for only a few days in the refrigerator, but you can also freeze them. Place them on a cookie sheet and freeze, then put them into a plastic freezer bag. They will last for a few months. Do not thaw before using them in soups, stews, sauces, and so forth.

**NUTS AND SEEDS** Toasting nuts before using them in a recipe has several advantages. First, it enhances the taste. Second, nuts that haven't been toasted tend to sink to the bottom of batter rather than staying suspended within it.

To toast nuts and seeds, place them on a cookie sheet and bake at 350°F for 8 to 20 minutes (depending on the nut), or until lightly browned.

### Nuts and Seeds

*If you want to be technical, a nut is the edible fruit from a tree or bush and is surrounded by a hard shell. Inside this shell is one edible kernel. According to this definition, the only "real" nuts are acorns, chestnuts, and hazelnuts. The other things that we consider nuts, such as almonds, cashews, macadamias, peanuts, pecans, pine nuts, and walnuts, are actually seeds.*

**ALMONDS** Unless you live in (or close to) California, you're not going to get local almonds. However, they ship well and can be stored for a long time. They can also be ground into flour or butter.

**PEANUTS** The peanut is actually a legume rather than a nut, as it grows underground. You can make your own peanut butter by grinding roasted nuts until they're creamy. Be aware that most commercial peanut butters are full of sugar and sweeteners. Peanuts are grown commercially in the Southeast and Southwest. They can also be grown in home gardens. Store peanuts in the refrigerator for up to nine months. Peanuts are often treated with very strong chemicals, so be sure that you purchase only organic nuts. Peanuts can trigger a severe allergic reaction in those who are sensitive.

**PECANS** These are among the few commercial nuts indigenous to the United States. In fact, pecans were part of the North American diet as far back as 8,000 years ago. They have a very high fat content. Store pecans in the refrigerator for up to six months and in the freezer for up to a year.

**WALNUTS** Walnut trees are relatively easy to grow in a home garden or orchard. The English walnut prefers a cool growing region, while the black walnut has a broader range and grows well in southern states. Because walnuts are often bleached and treated with various chemicals to extend their shelf life, be sure to purchase organic varieties. Store walnuts in a cool place for a few months or in the freezer for up to a year.

**PUMPKIN SEEDS** These are about the easiest of any of the seeds to obtain from a home garden or a local farmers' market. Varieties of pumpkins have been developed especially for their seed production. To roast your own pumpkin seeds, remove the seeds from the flesh of the pumpkin, wash off any stringy fibers, and dry with a towel. Spread them on a cookie sheet and roast in a 350°F oven for 15 minutes. Season with butter and salt.

**SUNFLOWER SEEDS** These are indigenous to the United States, although today Russia leads the world in the production of sunflower seeds. Also, like pumpkins, varieties of sunflowers have been developed specifically for seed production.

# MAPLE SUGAR ANGEL FOOD CAKE

¾ cup maple sugar

1½ cups cake flour

1½ teaspoons salt

14 large egg whites, at room temperature

1 teaspoon cream of tartar

½ cup maple syrup*

1½ teaspoons vanilla extract

¼ teaspoon almond extract

\* *original recipe called for 1¼ cups packed brown sugar instead of maple sugar and syrup*

**GMB Tip:** *This delicious, light cake makes a great base for many different sauces and ice creams. It's the perfect complement to something rich, such as the Maple Ice Cream (page 149) or Bev Shaffer's Rhubarb Compote (page 69).*

**Martha Hall Foose**

adapted with permission from *Screen Doors and Sweet Tea*

**FAT-FREE**

Serves 10 to 12

*This cake has a lovely ecru color and is perfect for tea parties, served with Lemon Curd Tart Filling (see page 173) and fresh berries. —Martha*

**1.** Preheat the oven to 350°F.

**2.** Put the maple sugar in a coffee grinder, a few tablespoons at a time. Pulse it several times, until it resembles flour. Combine the flour, ground maple sugar, and salt and sift twice onto a piece of wax or parchment paper.

**3.** Using an electric mixer, whip the egg whites on low speed until frothy. Add the cream of tartar, increase the mixer speed, and whip until the whites hold soft peaks.

**4.** In a small bowl, combine the maple syrup, vanilla extract, and almond extract.

**5.** Fold the maple syrup mixture into the whipped egg whites.

**6.** Transfer the whites to a large mixing bowl. **Note:** *Martha really does mean a LARGE bowl—the egg whites puff up to an amazing volume!* Sift the flour and maple sugar mixture over the whites in three additions, folding them in with a large, flat, rubber spatula.

**7.** Pour the batter into an ungreased 12-cup angel food cake pan (or Bundt pan). Bake for 20 minutes, or until the cake springs back when touched. Remove the pan from the oven, invert, and let the cake cool in the inverted pan. Run a thin knife around the sides of the pan. Release the cake and transfer it to a cake stand or serving platter.

# BAKED ALASKA

**CAKE BASE**

½ recipe of Debra Lynn Dadd's All-Organic Special Occasion Cake (see page 76) or the Green Market Baking Book Yellow Layer Cake (see page 33).

1 quart naturally sweetened ice cream (store-bought or homemade Maple Ice Cream [see page 149])

**MERINGUE**

4 egg whites

¼ teaspoon cream of tartar

½ tablespoon maple syrup

Serves 10 to 12

*This is my kids' favorite recipe, only it calls for natural sweeteners. It's a really impressive dessert, but not that hard to make. People who believe that naturally sweetened desserts can't be beautiful and sophisticated will be convinced otherwise by this dish.—GMB*

**1.** Bake the cake using two 8- or 9-inch round cake pans. Make it early in the day so it can cool completely. You need only one layer, so you'll have a layer left over, perfect for afternoon snacking, or frozen and saved for an unexpected celebration later on.

**2.** When the cake has cooled completely, slice one round in half horizontally, creating two thin round layers.

**3.** To assemble, cover a square piece of heavy cardboard, at least 12 inches across, with heavy aluminum foil. Cut a piece of parchment paper into a circle about 10 inches across. Put the parchment paper on the covered cardboard (the cardboard helps insulate the cake).

**4.** Carefully place one of the cake rounds on the parchment paper. Cover with half the ice cream. Cover it with plastic wrap and place in the freezer for one hour.

**5.** When chilled, place the remaining cake layer on top of the ice cream and top with a second layer of ice cream. Cover with plastic wrap and return it to the freezer for an additional 2 to 3 hours, or until frozen solid.

**6.** Preheat the oven to 425°F.

**7.** To make the meringue (just before serving), beat the egg whites until foamy, then turn off the mixer and add the cream of tartar and maple syrup.

**8.** Continue beating the egg whites until stiff and glossy.

**9.** Working quickly, cover the entire frozen cake with meringue. Be sure to seal the cake, completely covering it with the meringue.

**10.** Put the cake in the oven, watching it every second (egg whites will burn in a heartbeat)! Bake for about 3 or 4 minutes, or until the top is golden brown. Serve immediately.

# TOASTED ALMOND AND ORANGE CAKE WITH ORANGE GLAZE

## CAKE

- ¾ cup whole wheat pastry flour
- ¾ cup organic unbleached white flour
- ½ cup almonds, toasted and finely ground, divided
- 2 teaspoons non-aluminum baking powder
- ½ teaspoon five-spice powder or nutmeg
- ¼ teaspoon sea salt
- 2 tablespoons light almond oil (or any light vegetable oil)
- 6 tablespoons pure maple syrup
- 2 tablespoons brown rice syrup
- ¾ cup Edensoy plain soy milk
- Zest of half an orange
- ¼ cup orange juice
- ½ teaspoon vanilla extract
- ¼ teaspoon almond extract

### ORANGE GLAZE

- ½ cup (half a 10-ounce jar) fruit juice–sweetened marmalade
- 2 tablespoons water
- 2 teaspoons arrowroot

### Meredith McCarty

**DAIRY-FREE**

Makes 8 servings

*This little cake is inspired by one I had at a health retreat in Milan, Italy. It's easy to make and you can substitute any nuts and jams throughout the changing seasons.—Meredith*

### CAKE

**1.** Preheat the oven to 350°F. Line the bottom of a 9-inch cake pan with parchment paper, then brush the sides of the pan with oil.

**2.** In a large bowl, mix the dry ingredients. In a medium bowl, whisk the wet ingredients together and add them to the dry mixture. Whisk until the batter is almost smooth. Pour the batter into the pan.

**3.** Bake the cake for 30 minutes, or until a toothpick inserted into the center comes out clean. Allow the cake to cool in the pan for at least 10 minutes, then transfer it to a wire rack to cool completely.

**4.** Make the glaze while the cake cools. Spread the glaze evenly over the top of the cake, using the ground almonds as a garnish on the top.

### ORANGE GLAZE

Makes ⅔ cup

**1.** In a small saucepan whisk the ingredients together. Bring the mixture to a boil, whisking occasionally. Allow the glaze to firm up before using.

**Variation:** *Strawberry-Hazelnut Heart Cake: Substitute hazelnuts for almonds and strawberry jam for marmalade. Increase vanilla extract to 1 teaspoon and remove the almond extract. Bake in a 9-inch heart-shaped pan.*

# ORANGE-SCENTED CHOCOLATE CUPCAKES WITH CHOCOLATE FROSTING

## CUPCAKES

- 1½ cups whole wheat pastry flour
- ½ cup semolina flour
- ½ cup cocoa powder (preferably Dutch processed)
- 2 teaspoons baking powder
- Generous pinch of sea salt
- ½ cup avocado oil
- 1 cup brown rice syrup
- ¾ cup soy or almond milk
- 1 teaspoon brown rice vinegar
- 2 ounces non-dairy, grain-sweetened chocolate chips, coarsely chopped
- 2 teaspoons orange zest, plus extra for decoration

## CHOCOLATE FROSTING

- 1 cup non-dairy, grain-sweetened chocolate chips
- Scant ¼ cup soy or almond milk
- 2 teaspoons brown rice syrup

### Meredith McCarty

**DAIRY-FREE**

Makes 12 cupcakes

*Who doesn't love cupcakes? They're small enough to indulge in a whole one, sweet and decadent enough to feel like real treats, and so yummily comforting that they're my idea of the perfect food!—Meredith*

### CUPCAKES

**1.** Preheat the oven to 350°F and line a 12-cup muffin tin with liners.

**2.** Whisk together the flours, cocoa powder, baking powder, and sea salt.

**3.** In a separate bowl, whisk together the oil, rice syrup, soy or almond milk, and vinegar until smooth.

**4.** Mix the wet ingredients into the dry mixture to create a smooth batter.

**5.** Fold in the chopped chocolate and orange peel, spoon evenly into muffin cups, and bake for 20 to 25 minutes.

**6.** Remove the cupcakes from the oven and allow them to cool on a wire rack.

**7.** Make the Chocolate Frosting while the cupcakes cool. Spread the frosting over the top of each cupcake, garnishing with a sprinkle of orange peel.

### CHOCOLATE FROSTING

**1.** Place the chocolate in a heat-resistant bowl. Bring the soy or almond milk and rice syrup to a rolling boil and pour it over the chocolate.

**2.** Whisk until the chocolate mixture is thick and smooth. Cover the bowl loosely and set it aside for 30 to 40 minutes to allow the frosting to set.

**3.** Whisk again to loosen the frosting before use.

# MEXICAN CHOCOLATE CAKE WITH VEGAN MEXICAN GANACHE OR CINNAMON CREAM CHEESE MAPLE ICING

2¼ cups all-purpose unbleached flour

½ cup dark cocoa powder

1½ teaspoons baking soda

½ teaspoon cayenne pepper

1 teaspoon cinnamon

½ teaspoon salt

1 cup brown rice syrup

1 cup unsweetened applesauce

¾ cup vegetable oil

1 tablespoon vanilla extract

1 cup strong brewed hot coffee

2 tablespoons apple cider vinegar

**To make this cake wheat-free:** *Replace flours with 2¼ cups wheat-free flours (try a blend of rice, sorghum, and garbanzo flours, but any are fine to use) and 2¼ teaspoons xanthan gum. Make it exactly like the original recipe. The wheat-free replacement makes an already moist cake even moister. You may want to go just a few minutes past the "toothpick comes out clean" stage in the oven.*

## Jodi Rhoden

**VEGAN**

Makes two 8-inch round layers or 18 cupcakes

*This vegan Mexican Chocolate Cake is one of my customers' favorites. Because there's no butterfat, the flavor of the chocolate and spice really comes through—it's a very rich, chocolaty, moist cake. There are so many variations you can create in terms of icing flavors, sizes of cake layers, and design styles and decorations. I like to make the recipe into cupcakes and decorate with Day of the Dead toppers for a fiesta theme. Enjoy!—Jodi*

### MEXICAN CHOCOLATE CAKE

**1.** Preheat the oven to 350°F. Butter and line two 8-inch cake pans with parchment paper, or prepare muffin pans with paper liners.

**2.** Place the dry ingredients in a large mixing bowl and whisk together.

**3.** In a separate bowl, mix the rice syrup, applesauce, vegetable oil, and vanilla extract. Then add the hot coffee and vinegar and blend. Add the wet mixture to the dry ingredients and mix until everything is combined.

**4.** Quickly pour the batter in the baking pans or muffin pans and bake for 20 to 30 minutes, or until the cake comes away from the sides of the pans and a toothpick inserted into the center comes out clean.

**GMB Tip:** *For a beautiful rounded cake, we baked the cake in a 10-inch metal mixing bowl for about 45 minutes, then poured the still-runny ganache over it. To do this, we placed the cake on top of an upside-down glass pie pan before pouring the ganache over it.*

# VEGAN MEXICAN GANACHE
# OR CINNAMON CREAM CHEESE MAPLE ICING

**VEGAN MEXICAN GANACHE**

1 package silken firm tofu

2 cups melted grain-sweetened chocolate chips

½ teaspoon cayenne pepper (optional)

1 teaspoon cinnamon (optional)

**CINNAMON CREAM CHEESE MAPLE ICING**

1 package cream cheese, at room temperature

½ stick butter

½ cup maple syrup

2 teaspoons cinnamon

**VEGAN MEXICAN GANACHE**

**VEGAN**

**1.** In a food processor with the blade attachment, puree all the ingredients. Cool until the ganache is thick enough to pour over the cake, or cool even longer to spread with a knife.

**CINNAMON CREAM CHEESE MAPLE ICING**

**1.** Cream together the cream cheese and butter. Add the maple syrup and cinnamon. Refrigerate. Pipe onto the cupcakes, or use to ice the cake.

**GMB Tip:** *To make this vegan, take out the cream cheese and butter and substitute with one 8-ounce container of Tofutti brand imitation cream cheese and 2 ounces of Earth Balance margarine.*

# CHOCOLATE COCONUT COOKIES

½ cup grain-sweetened bittersweet or semisweet chocolate chips

2 large egg whites

Pinch of sea salt

½ cup maple sugar

½ teaspoon vanilla extract

1 cup unsweetened coconut

3 tablespoons cocoa powder, sifted

**GMB Tip:** *Remember that grain-sweetened chocolate chips are not guaranteed to be gluten-free.*

### Susan Baldassano

**WHEAT-FREE**

Makes 14 to 16 cookies

*Oh, boy! These are tasty, easy-to-make morsels. Be sure that you find unsweetened coconut (most coconut is packed with sugar).—GMB*

**1.** Preheat the oven to 350°F. Line a cookie sheet with parchment paper.

**2.** Place the chocolate chips in the double boiler. Melt the chocolate and set it aside to cool.

**3.** In a medium bowl, add the egg whites and salt and beat with an electric mixer. Slowly add the maple sugar until the mixture forms soft peaks.

**4.** Using a spatula, fold in the vanilla extract and coconut.

**5.** Add the cocoa powder and melted chocolate. Gently stir to incorporate all the ingredients.

**6.** Using a 1-ounce ice cream scoop, scoop out cookies onto the cookie sheet, leaving room for a slight spread. Bake 15 to 20 minutes. Cool and serve.

# CHOCOLATE PEANUT BUTTER COOKIES

⅓ cup Earth Balance butter substitute

½ cup brown rice syrup

⅓ cup unsweetened crunchy peanut butter

1 teaspoon pure vanilla extract

1½ cups whole wheat pastry flour

½ cup quick rolled oats

Pinch of sea salt

Pinch of ground cinnamon (optional)

¼ cup unsweetened almond milk, or as needed

1 cup non-dairy, grain-sweetened chocolate chips

## Christina Pirello

**DAIRY-FREE**

Makes 2 dozen cookies

*Chocolate and peanut butter come together to create a decadent-tasting cookie, but without the guilt!—Christina*

**1.** Preheat the oven to 350°F. Line two baking sheets with unbleached parchment paper or silicone baking sheets.

**2.** Combine the butter substitute, syrup, and peanut butter in a small saucepan over low heat. Cook, whisking constantly, for about 3 minutes, or until the mixture is smooth and creamy. Remove from the heat and whisk in the vanilla extract. Set the pan aside to cool to room temperature.

**3.** Mix together the flour, oats, salt, and cinnamon (if using). Mix the wet ingredients into the dry ingredients to form a spoonable batter. If it is too thick or too dry, add some unsweetened almond milk. Fold in the chocolate chips until they are well incorporated.

**4.** With wet hands, roll tablespoons of the dough into balls and place them onto the baking sheets. Press a wet fork into each cookie crosswise, creating a crosshatch pattern in center.

**5.** Bake for 12 to 15 minutes, then allow the cookies to stand on the hot baking sheets for 2 minutes. Transfer to a wire cooling rack to cool completely.

# HONEY FIG BARS

1¼ cups honey, divided

½ cup butter, at room
temperature

1 egg

1 cup all-purpose flour

2 cups whole wheat flour

1 teaspoon baking powder

½ teaspoon baking soda

1 pound dried figs (about
2¼ cups, chopped)

2 tablespoons lemon juice

2 teaspoons lemon zest

½ cup chopped pecans
or walnuts (optional)

**National Honey Board**
Makes 16 bars

*If you like Fig Newtons, you'll absolutely love these honey fig bars. A
delicate cookie dough surrounds a yummy filling of honey, figs, and
chopped nuts. They are healthful, not too sweet, and the perfect cookie
to have with a glass of milk.—GMB*

**1.** In a medium bowl, cream ¾ cup of the honey with the
butter until light and fluffy. Beat in the egg.

**2.** Add the flour, baking powder, and baking soda and
combine. Wrap the dough in plastic wrap and refrigerate it
for about 2 hours, until firm (or overnight).

**3.** Meanwhile, in the bowl of a food processor with a
metal blade, combine the remaining ½ cup of honey, the
figs, lemon juice, lemon zest, and chopped nuts (if using).
Process until the figs are finely chopped. Set aside.

**4.** When the dough is well chilled, dust a work surface and
the dough with some flour. Working quickly, roll the dough
to ¼ inch thick. With a sharp knife, trim the dough into
two 14×6-inch rectangles. Dough trimmings can be used to
make cutout cookies. **Note:** *The original recipe called for two
12×3-inch rectangles. However, we found that we had enough
dough to make much larger rectangles, which were easier to work
with. It also allowed for more filling and less dough per cookie.*

**5.** Spread half the fig mixture evenly down the center of one dough rectangle. Gently fold the right side of the rectangle over the filling, then fold the left side over the right so they overlap. Pinch the ends to seal. Repeat with the remaining rectangle and the fig mixture. Carefully place the dough logs seam-side down on a greased baking sheet.

**6.** Bake at 350°F for about 15 minutes, or until the logs are lightly browned. Remove the cookie sheet from the oven, allowing the logs to cool for 5 minutes on the sheet. Transfer the cookies to a wire rack to cool completely. Cut into 3-inch bars.

> **GMB Tip:** *Try cutting the bars into pieces about 3 inches by 1 inch. For parties (or for younger kids), cut these bars in half.*

# COCONUT DATE ROLLS

2 cups fresh pitted dates, such as the Medjool variety

1 cup unsweetened shredded coconut

**Alexandra Jamieson**

from *The Great American Detox Diet*

**DAIRY-FREE** **WHEAT-FREE**

Makes 20 small rolls

*You've probably seen something like these fabulous coconut date rolls in your local natural foods grocery store. Make them yourself for a fraction of the cost! They are good for you, easy to make, and delicious. Enjoy!—GMB*

**1.** In a food processor, chop the dates by pulsing 20 times.

**2.** In a mixing bowl, combine the dates and coconut with a wooden spoon.

**3.** Spoon out 2 tablespoons at a time and roll the dough into log shapes with your hands.

**4.** Store in an airtight container in the refrigerator for up to a week. Serve cold or at room temperature.

**GMB Tip:** *If you can't find fresh dates, use dried dates. They'll still be delicious!*

# CHOCOLATE HONEY TART

## CRUST

18 small Graham Crackers (see page 51), crumbled (about 1¼ cups)*

3 tablespoons unsalted butter, divided, at room temperature

1 tablespoon honey

* *original recipe called for 9 whole chocolate graham crackers, about 5 ounces*

## FILLING

1 cup whipping cream

2 teaspoons dried lavender blossoms (optional)

12 ounces grain-sweetened chocolate chips*

1 tablespoon unsweetened cocoa powder

1 tablespoon butter

* *original recipe called for 12 ounces bittersweet or semisweet chocolate chips*

**Note:** *This recipe can be made 1 day ahead. Cover the tart and keep it chilled. Let it stand at room temperature for 1 hour before serving.*

**Rozanne Gold**

Serves 10 to 12

*The lavender adds a floral flavor to this tart, which you may or may not want. If not, just leave out the lavender.—Rozanne*

**1.** Preheat the oven to 350°F.

**2.** To make the crust, grease a 9-inch tart pan with a removable bottom. Grind the graham crackers with the butter and honey in a food processor until fine crumbs form. Press the crumbs evenly onto the bottom (but not the sides) of a prepared tart pan. Bake for about 10 minutes, or until the crust is set. Cool.

**3.** To make the filling, bring the cream and lavender just to a boil in a small saucepan. Reduce the heat to low and simmer for 5 minutes.

**4.** Place the chocolate in a medium saucepan, then strain the hot cream mixture onto the chocolate. Stir over medium-low heat just until melted and smooth. Add the cocoa powder and remaining 1 tablespoon of butter; stir until the mixture is melted and smooth.

**5.** Pour the chocolate filling into the graham cracker crust. Chill for at least 45 minutes (the chocolate will be slightly soft after 45 minutes and firm after 2 hours). Cut into wedges and serve.

**GMB Tip:** *We loved this sophisticated, very chocolaty dessert. We thought it was even more decadent when served at room temperature. For a special party treat, cut it into small wedges, then add a dollop of whipped cream and a tiny piece of seasonal fruit.*

# CHOCOLATE TOFU PUDDING

1 package silken tofu

1 10-ounce package grain-sweetened dark chocolate chips, such as Sunspire brand

3 tablespoons agave syrup

1 teaspoon vanilla extract

Pinch of sea salt

**Alexandra Jamieson**

from *The Great American Detox Diet* (Rodale, 2005)

**DAIRY-FREE**

Makes 3 cups

*If you—or your children—are in the mood for something yummy and chocolaty (but not bad for you!), this is the recipe for you. The texture is as creamy and smooth as the best pudding you've ever eaten.—GMB*

**1.** Line a mesh sieve with paper towels and place the tofu inside. Cover the tofu with paper towels, and weigh it down, either with an unopened can laid sideways or with two or three stacked bowls. Allow the tofu to drain for 15 minutes, or until about ⅓ cup of liquid has drained out.

**2.** Blend the tofu in a food processor or blender until just smooth.

**3.** In a double boiler, soften the chocolate chips with the agave syrup over low heat. Stir gently with a rubber spatula until the chocolate is melted.

**4.** Add the chocolate mixture to the tofu in the food processor or blender. Add the vanilla extract and salt and mix until creamy, scraping down the sides once or twice to ensure complete incorporation.

**5.** Scrape the pudding into an airtight glass container and refrigerate for at least 1 hour, until set.

# QUINOA PUDDING

½ cup maple sugar

2 tablespoons butter, softened, plus extra for greasing pan

2 eggs

1 cup milk

1 tablespoon vanilla extract

1 teaspoon cinnamon

Pinch of sea salt

2 cups cooked quinoa

½ cup chopped toasted hazelnuts

½ cup currants

Freshly grated nutmeg to taste

## Rebecca Wood

**WHEAT-FREE**

Serves 4 to 6

*Similar to rice pudding, quinoa pudding is both more delicate and more substantial. This whole-grain, wheat-free dessert is so healthy and satisfying that some people eat it for breakfast! May you be well nourished.—Rebecca*

**1.** Preheat the oven to 350°F.

**2.** Cream the sugar and butter. Stir in the eggs, milk, vanilla extract, cinnamon, and salt until blended.

**3.** Add the quinoa, hazelnuts, and currants and mix thoroughly. Butter a 1½-quart casserole or soufflé dish (or 6 individual ramekins).

**4.** Pour the custard mixture into the casserole dish or ramekins and grate a little nutmeg over it. Bake for 40 minutes, or until just set. (Or, as an alternative method, steam, covered, in the top of a double boiler over boiling water for about 1 hour.)

**5.** To serve, spoon the pudding from the casserole dish or ramekins onto individual plates, or loosen the edges with a knife and invert the pudding(s) onto a serving platter (or individual plates).

# LEMON RASPBERRY TART

1 cup unbleached all-purpose flour

1 cup whole wheat pastry flour

½ teaspoon salt

½ cup butter plus 1 tablespoon, very cold

¼ cup water

1 recipe Lemon Curd Tart filling (follows)

1 cup whipping cream

1 cup fresh raspberries

**GMB Tip:** *If you don't have tart pans, you can use a muffin pan.*

Makes three 6-inch or six 3-inch tartlets

*A sugar version of this dish was very popular at the New York Metropolitan Opera restaurant. It was one of the most beautiful, sophisticated desserts they offered and is the perfect way to end a beautiful meal. Our favorite Lemon Curd recipe is contributed by Melissa Breyer.—GMB*

**1.** To make the crust, in a food processor, mix the flours and salt. Add the very cold butter by the tablespoon.

**2.** Pulse the processor until the butter is mixed with the flour, but still in marble-size pieces. Add the water, then pulse until the mixture becomes a soft dough.

**3.** Divide the dough into two pieces, wrap it in plastic, and chill it for at least 30 minutes.

**4.** Place the dough on a floured surface and roll to ¼-inch thick.

**5.** Preheat the oven to 350°F.

**6.** Divide the dough into four equal rounds, each one large enough to line a tartlet pan. Chill again for 15 minutes. After chilling, roll out each piece and put it in a tart pan. Use a fork to poke holes in the dough.

**7.** Prebake the crust by weighing down the dough with either dried beans, baking beans, or another tart pan. Bake for 10 minutes, or until the edges of the crust are brown and there are no wet spots. Take the weights off the crust and bake for another 5 to 7 minutes or until the crust is a consistent golden brown. Let cool.

**8.** Make Melissa Breyer's Lemon Curd Filling (see next page) and fill tarts.

**9.** To make the topping, beat the whipping cream until soft peaks form. Put a dollop of the topping onto the cooled tartlets, then top with raspberries and serve.

# LEMON CURD TART FILLING

5 large organic egg yolks

1 large organic egg

⅔ cup fresh organic lemon juice

⅓ cup honey

4 tablespoons unsalted butter, cut into small pieces

1 tablespoon finely grated organic lemon zest

**Melissa Breyer**

*Give me a bolt of sour with my sweet, and I am very happy. Say the words "lemon curd" and a joyous little yelp may escape from my lips. Lemon curd has many applications: It can be spread on scones or biscuits, used in tarts (such as the one on the opposite page), layered in cakes, rolled in pancakes, or simply eaten with a spoon.—Melissa*

**1.** In a medium stainless steel bowl, whisk together the egg yolks and egg with the lemon juice and honey.

**2.** Place the bowl over a pot of simmering water and cook the egg mixture, whisking constantly, for 7 to 10 minutes, or until it becomes pale and thickened.

**3.** Remove the bowl from the heat and immediately pour the egg mixture through a fine strainer to remove any lumps. Whisk in the butter until it has melted.

**4.** Stir in the lemon zest, cover with wax paper, and cool to room temperature.

# LEMON RICOTTA PANCAKES
## WITH BLUEBERRIES

2 cups ricotta (about 1 pound)

4 large eggs, separated

Zest of 1 lemon

Pinch of salt

Dash of pure vanilla extract

2 tablespoons honey*

1 cup all-purpose flour

7 tablespoons unsalted butter, melted, plus additional butter to cook pancakes

1½ cups fresh or frozen blueberries

Maple syrup, warmed

* *original recipe called for 2 tablespoons sugar*

**U.S. Highbush Blueberry Council**
Serves 4

*A great, tasty pancake perfect for a family gathering or a fancy brunch. The lemon zest adds a great bit of flavor and is a wonderful complement to the blueberries. You can make this any time of the year, substituting seasonal fruits such as raspberries, huckleberries, or any other kind of berries. If you don't have fresh berries, use frozen ones.—GMB*

**1.** Set an oven-safe platter or baking sheet with a cooling rack on top of it into the oven, and turn the oven to 200°F.

**2.** Beat the ricotta and egg yolks together in a large mixing bowl with the lemon zest, salt, vanilla extract, and honey. Stir in the flour and 7 tablespoons of melted butter, working the batter until just combined.

**3.** Whip the egg whites with a whisk or handheld mixer until stiff peaks form. With a rubber spatula, gingerly fold half of the whites into the batter, then fold in the remaining half. Don't worry if the resulting batter is lightly striped with whipped whites—they'll make the pancakes light and airy.

**4.** Heat a large cast-iron or nonstick skillet or griddle over medium-low heat for 1 or 2 minutes, then grease the pan with a teaspoon or more of the remaining butter. When the butter starts to sizzle, turn the heat up slightly and ladle in enough batter to make 3½- to 4-inch pancakes. Add a sprinkling of blueberries to each pancake.

**5.** After several minutes, when the bottoms of the pancakes are somewhere between mottled and uniformly brown, flip them and cook for another 2 minutes. Transfer the finished pancakes to a platter in the oven and repeat with the remaining batter. Put the serving plates in the oven to warm them before adding the last of the batter to the pan.

**6.** Serve the pancakes on warmed plates, with warmed maple syrup on the side.

# BOB'S FAVORITE SCOTTISH OATCAKES

1½ cups Bob's Red Mill Scottish Oatmeal, divided

½ cup whole wheat pastry flour

¾ teaspoon honey*

¼ teaspoon sea salt

¼ teaspoon baking powder

¼ cup butter, melted

½ cup hot water

* *original recipe called for ¾ teaspoon turbinado sugar*

## Bob's Red Mill
Makes 12 oatcakes

*These little cakes are perfect for on-the-go breakfasts, or for leisurely ones. They are the perfect accompaniment to a pot of tea and are great just as they are or with a little butter and homemade jam. This is Bob Moore's favorite recipe.—GMB*

1. Preheat the oven to 325°F.

2. Place all but two tablespoons of the oatmeal in a bowl with the flour, honey, salt, and baking powder; stir until combined. Add the butter and stir until it is evenly distributed. With a fork, mix in the water until just moistened. Pat the dough into a ball, then flatten it slightly.

3. Sprinkle the reserved 2 tablespoons of oats on the work surface. Roll the dough out to ¼ inch thick.

4. Cut the dough with a 2- to 3-inch round cutter. Reroll and cut the scraps. Place the oatcakes about ¼ inch apart on a greased baking sheet.

5. Bake for approximately 25 minutes, or until the oatcakes are golden. Let the oatcakes cool on a wire rack. Enjoy them plain, served with jam or cheese, or use them to build hors d'oeuvres.

# FLYING BISCUIT MAPLE SYRUP JOHNNYCAKES WITH FREE RANGE CHICKEN SAUSAGE GRAVY

## JOHNNYCAKES

- 2 cups (approximately 2 ears) fresh sweet corn
- 2 cups yellow cornmeal
- 1 cup all-purpose flour, sifted
- 1 tablespoon baking power
- ¾ teaspoon salt
- ½ cup (1 stick) unsalted butter, cut into small pieces, at room temperature
- 1½ cups milk
- 3 large eggs
- 1 cup maple syrup

**GMB Tip:** *When we first made this, it took almost an hour to bake and was very thick. For a thinner cake and shorter baking time, use a bigger pan, such as a 9×13-inch baking pan.*

**Delia Champion**

Serves 12

*Small, flat cornmeal cakes go by a variety of names, depending on cooking methods and locale. They are known as johnnycakes, ashcakes, battercakes, corn cakes, corn pone, hoecakes, Shawnee cakes, or journey cakes. The original recipe for johnnycakes (and its cousins) is very old. Native Americans probably showed the early settlers how to grind corn into meal and cook it over an open fire to make the first versions of this cake. Here Delia combines fresh browned corn and maple syrup to create an astonishingly delicious cornmeal cake. Although this recipe calls for the batter to bake in the oven, you can also make individual cakes on a griddle with the same batter or cook it over an open fire, if you so desire. Any way you do it, this is a fabulous cornbread.—GMB*

**1.** Preheat the oven to 350°F. Butter the bottom of a 9×9-inch baking dish.

**2.** To make the johnnycakes, in a dry (no oil) nonstick skillet over medium-high heat, sauté the corn until it is tender and starts to brown.

**3.** Combine the dry ingredients in a bowl. Add the butter and mix until the mixture resembles coarse meal.

**4.** In a separate bowl, whisk together the milk, eggs, maple syrup, and corn.

**5.** Pour the liquid mixture into the dry mixture and stir with a wooden spoon until just barely incorporated. Do not overmix.

**6.** Transfer to the baking dish and bake for approximately 25 minutes, or until a toothpick inserted into the center comes out clean.

# FREE RANGE CHICKEN SAUSAGE GRAVY

1 pound free range chicken sausage

1 large diced onion

2 cloves garlic

1 teaspoon dried rosemary

1 teaspoon thyme

2 tablespoons chopped parsley

3 teaspoons ground black pepper

½ cup (1 stick) unsalted butter

¼ cup all-purpose flour

8 cups heavy cream

2 cups half-and-half (or some combination of cream, milk, and half-and-half)

Cayenne pepper

Salt

Serves 12

*No one ever accused Southerners of "going lite." This is an incredibly rich and unbelievably delicious gravy—great over the johnnycakes and equally good over biscuits. Indulge. Savor. Enjoy. Exercise.—GMB*

**1.** Brown the sausage in a large pot. While it's cooking, chop the sausage into medium-sized pieces with a spoon. Make sure the sausage is cooked completely.

**2.** Remove the pot from the stove and drain the fat off the sausage. Remove the sausage and set aside. In the same pot, sauté the onions, garlic, rosemary, thyme, parsley, and black pepper in the butter.

**3.** Add the flour to the sausage and stir until mixed completely. Add the sausage back to the pot. Stir well. Add the cream and half-and-half.

**4.** Stir and simmer over low heat. Cook to desired thickness. Add cayenne pepper and salt to taste.

**GMB Tip:** *For a gravy that is not quite as rich, use a combination of whole milk and half-and-half, gradually added. We used 4 cups of whole milk and 2 cups of half-and-half. Add reduced-fat milk to thin the gravy if it becomes too thick.*

# SPELT SCONES

2½ cups organic spelt flour

1½ teaspoons baking powder

½ teaspoon baking soda

¼ teaspoon sea salt

6 tablespoons unsalted butter, softened

1 organic egg

½ cup organic buttermilk

¼ cup barley malt syrup

½ cup maple syrup*

1 teaspoon pure vanilla extract

* *original recipe called for ½ cup Sucanat*

**Melissa Breyer**
Makes 8 scones

*In this recipe, spelt flour and buttermilk are used in place of white flour and cream, and the result is as crumbly and velvety as anyone could dream a scone to be. This is a very basic recipe, quite amenable to additions. Currants are classic, but dried cherries or blueberries can be a nice surprise. Savory flavors work well, too, if you omit the sweetener and vanilla extract. Rosemary and sea salt? Yum.—Melissa*

**1.** Preheat the oven to 400°F and line an ungreased baking pan with parchment paper.

**2.** Combine the spelt flour, baking powder, baking soda, and salt in a large bowl. Add the butter and, with a pastry blender or two knives, cut the butter in until it is well combined and the mixture resembles coarse crumbs.

**3.** In a separate bowl, lightly beat the egg and whisk in the buttermilk, sweeteners, and vanilla extract. Add the egg mixture to the flour mixture and gently combine.

**4.** Drop the mixture into 8 balls on the baking pan, several inches apart (they will expand).

**5.** Bake 17 to 20 minutes, until golden, or until a toothpick inserted into the center comes out clean.

**GMB Tip:** *We added blueberries and they were fabulous!*

# CARAMELIZED ONION AND BLUE CHEESE TART

1 tablespoon unsalted butter

2 tablespoons olive oil

2 medium onions, very thinly sliced

1 teaspoon sea salt

¼ teaspoon pepper

1 teaspoon chopped fresh thyme, plus 1 tablespoon whole leaves for garnish

2 tablespoons balsamic vinegar

1 14-ounce package puff pastry, defrosted in refrigerator when ready to use

½ cup (2 ounces) blue cheese, crumbled

**GMB Tip:** *Serve this in small squares as hors d'oeuvres with aperitifs, or in larger wedges with lightly dressed greens for a satisfying first course or light meal.*

**Nicki Sizemore**

Serves 8 to 12

*With sweet balsamic-laced caramelized onions, salty blue cheese, buttery puff pastry, and a hint of fresh thyme, this rustic tart is as simple as it is mouthwatering. It can be pulled together year-round with ingredients that always seem to be on hand, making it perfect for last-minute entertaining. —Nicki*

**1.** Preheat the oven to 400°F. Line a large baking sheet with parchment paper or spray with cooking spray.

**2.** In a large skillet over medium heat, melt the butter and olive oil. Add the sliced onions, salt, and pepper; stir well to coat the onions in the oil. Cook about 18 to 22 minutes, stirring often, until the onions are dark golden in color. Add the chopped thyme and cook for 30 seconds. Add the balsamic vinegar and scrape up any browned bits on the bottom of the pan. Stir until the vinegar is completely distributed and absorbed. Transfer the caramelized onions to a bowl. **Note:** *The onions can be covered and refrigerated for up to 3 days. Bring to room temperature before proceeding with the recipe.*

**3.** On a lightly floured surface, roll out the puff pastry to ⅛-inch thick. Transfer to the baking sheet. Brush the edges of the pastry with water and fold it over to create a 1-inch rim. Using a fork, poke the dough all over (except on the rim).

**4.** Bake the pastry for 15 minutes, or until it is light golden and puffed. Remove the pan from the oven and arrange the onions evenly over the top (inside the rim), deflating the puff in the middle. Scatter the cheese over the onions. Bake 20 to 22 minutes longer, or until the pastry is deep golden brown around the edges. Turn the oven off, but leave the tart inside for 10 more minutes, allowing the pastry to dry out slightly.

**5.** Let the tart cool for 5 minutes. Sprinkle with fresh thyme. Serve warm or at room temperature.

# SOFT PRETZELS

1 tablespoon agave nectar

3 cups warm water, divided

1 packet active dry yeast

2 to 3 cups unbleached all-purpose flour, divided

1 teaspoon salt

2 tablespoons light olive oil*

2 tablespoons baking soda

2 tablespoons coarse salt

* *original recipe called for 2 tablespoons canola oil*

**Colleen Patrick-Goudreau**

**DAIRY-FREE**

Makes 12 large pretzels or 24 sticks

*These come out just the way pretzels were meant to be eaten: crispy on the outside and fluffy on the inside.—Colleen*

**1.** Stir the agave nectar into the warm water. Once it has been evenly distributed, add the yeast and allow it to dissolve, then whisk and let sit for 10 minutes. Yeast should look foamy on the surface.

**2.** Add the oil to the yeast mixture.

**3.** In a large mixing bowl, mix 2 cups of the flour and the salt. Make a well in the center and add the yeast mixture. Stir until the ingredients are well combined, continuing to add more flour as needed. **Note:** *We used about 2¼ cups to 2½ cups flour total.*

**4.** When the dough is easy to handle, knead it for about 3 minutes, then form it into a ball.

**5.** Place the dough in a bowl lightly coated with oil. Cover with plastic wrap and a damp cloth and let it sit for about 2 hours in a warm, draft-free spot to rise. The dough should double in size.

**6.** Divide the dough into 12 pieces and roll each piece into a ball (dust hands with flour to prevent sticking). Place the balls on a cookie sheet or a lightly floured surface. Let rest for about 10 minutes.

**7.** Lightly grease a large baking sheet or line it with parchment paper to prevent sticking.

**8.** Preheat the oven to 400° F.

**9.** Roll each ball into a rope, 16 inches in length, and form it into a pretzel or other fun shapes. **Note:** *We couldn't get our dough to roll out nearly this long but found that shorter pieces made great pretzel shapes anyway*!

**10.** In a large bowl, dissolve the baking soda in the remaining 2 cups of water. Carefully dip the shaped pretzels in water. Shake off any excess water and place each pretzel on the cookie sheet. Sprinkle each pretzel with coarse salt.

**11.** Bake for 15 to 20 minutes, or until golden brown. They're best eaten right out of the oven, but you can freeze them for up to a month and reheat later at 375°F for 5 minutes.

# ROSEMARY OLIVE BREAD

1 ounce fresh yeast (or 2 teaspoons dry yeast)

1 cup warm water

4 tablespoons extra virgin olive oil

1¼ teaspoons kosher salt

3½ cups organic bread flour

½ cup chopped kalamata olives, pitted

2 tablespoons chopped fresh rosemary

### Linton Hopkins

**DAIRY-FREE**

Makes 1 free-formed loaf

*This tasty, savory bread is a wonderful way to use fresh rosemary, either from your garden or from a market. The olives add a tangy surprise that keeps you wanting more. This is fabulous served with a good olive oil.—GMB*

**1.** Dissolve the yeast in the warm water.

**2.** Add the olive oil and salt to the yeast and water.

**3.** Add 3 cups of the flour, the olives, and the rosemary.

**4.** Gradually add more flour until you can work the dough.

**5.** Knead for 8 to 10 minutes, or until a tight ball forms.

**6.** Place the dough in a large bowl, cover, and let it rise for 1 to 2 hours, or until doubled in size.

**7.** Punch down, shape, and let the dough rise again for 30 minutes.

**8.** Bake at 350°F for 20 to 30 minutes, or until the loaf is golden brown and cooked through.

# CRANBERRY COCONUT GRANOLA

5 cups old-fashioned rolled oats

1 cup wheat germ

½ cup flaxseed meal (ground flaxseeds)

1 cup unsweetened shredded coconut

½ cup raw pumpkin seeds

½ cup raw almonds

1 teaspoon ground cinnamon

1½ teaspoons salt

⅓ cup extra virgin, unrefined coconut oil

½ cup raw honey (or ¼ cup raw honey plus ¼ cup maple syrup)

1 teaspoon vanilla extract

¼ teaspoon almond extract

½ cup boiling water

½ cup dried cranberries

## Nicole Sizemore

**DAIRY-FREE** **WHEAT-FREE**

Serves 8 to 12

*For me, there are few aromas as enticing or welcoming as homemade granola baking in the oven—toasted oats and nuts, warm cinnamon, vanilla, honey, and, here, a hint of coconut . . . irresistible. This healthful recipe is packed with wholesome ingredients, comes together easily, and makes a big enough batch to last weeks. Feel free to swap out the almonds and cranberries for your favorite nuts and dried fruit. Enjoy it with yogurt or milk for an ideal breakfast, or sprinkled over roasted fruit with a dollop of unsweetened or naturally sweetened whipped cream for a delicious dessert.—Nicole*

**1.** Preheat the oven to 300°F. In a large bowl, mix together the oats, wheat germ, flaxseed meal, shredded coconut, pumpkin seeds, almonds, cinnamon, and salt.

**2.** In a small bowl, mix together the coconut oil, honey (or honey and maple syrup), vanilla extract, almond extract, and boiling water. Whisk until ingredients are well combined.

**3.** Pour the wet ingredients over the dry mixture and stir until all the dry ingredients are evenly coated. Spread the mixture onto one large (or two small) rimmed baking sheet(s) and bake for 30 to 45 minutes, stirring every 15 minutes, until toasted and golden. Cool completely, then stir in cranberries. Store the granola at room temperature in an airtight container for up to 3 weeks.

# HONEY CRANBERRY SAUCE

1 cup apple cider (or apple juice)

½ cup honey

¼ cup maple syrup

2 cinnamon sticks, broken in half

1 tablespoon orange zest

3 whole cloves

3 cups fresh cranberries (or one 12-ounce bag cranberries)

2 pears (Anjou or Bartlett), peeled and cut into bite-sized pieces

Pinch of salt

Makes 2½ cups

*This new version of an old-fashioned holiday favorite is great with meats, such as chicken, pork, or turkey, but is also wonderful on toast or muffins in the morning. This has even more flavor than traditional cranberry sauce, but none of the cloying sweetness.—GMB*

**1.** In a saucepan over low heat, combine the cider (or juice), honey, maple syrup, spices, and orange zest. Cook for 5 to 7 minutes.

**2.** Turn off the heat and allow the sauce to sit for about 30 minutes, then remove the cinnamon sticks and cloves.

**3.** Put the saucepan back on the stove and add the cranberries and pears.

**4.** Cook until the cranberries begin to burst and the pears are tender, about 6 minutes. Cool, then serve.

# Preserving the Harvest

I LOVE USING FRESH, SEASONAL PRODUCE—THERE IS SIMPLY NOTHING better than eating something you've picked right off the vine. Warmed by the sun, touched by a gentle breeze, and washed clean by the rain, the local fruits of the earth offer a taste that can't be surpassed by farther-flung options.

Unfortunately, that fresh-from-the-farm experience is not always (okay, not nearly often enough) available to us. The next best thing is to capture as much of it as you can by preserving, and there are several ways that you can do this. Preserving food is an art and a craft, but with the right information, you can enjoy the abundance of the harvest throughout the year.

The three main methods of preserving food at home are canning, freezing, and drying. Different fruits and vegetables are suited to different methods, and sometimes even different varieties of the same vegetable will best be preserved by different methods, meaning you need to know your produce before you start slicing and dicing.

In general, fresh, young, and tender produce is best preserved by freezing, while riper, more mature fruits and vegetables do better when they are canned. Dried foods, made with fully ripe produce, also allow you to enjoy the fruits of the farm and garden during the off-season. Produce that has seen better days—meaning soft, squishy, and overripe—should be eaten or discarded. Unlike a good wine, the taste of a tomato, for example, does not improve with age, no matter how well preserved.

· · · · · · ·

## Freezing

The appropriate container is critical to preserving freshness. Choose containers that are easy to seal, that are moisture-resistant, and that do not become brittle at very low temperatures. Plastic freezer bags (not "sandwich" or "storage" bags), plastic containers that are marked suitable for freezing, and wide-mouthed glass canning jars (not regular glass jars) are all great for storing produce in the freezer.

When harvesting, try to pick produce in the cool of the morning when everything is full of moisture, and process as quickly after picking as possible.

The following chart gives you some idea of preferred preservation methods for a few common fruits and vegetables:

| Produce | Can | Freeze | Dry | Notes |
|---------|-----|--------|-----|-------|
| Apples | yes | yes | yes | Freeze for baked goods; can for applesauce. |
| Berries | yes | yes | yes | Good for baking. |
| Corn | | blanch first | | Blanch 9 minutes for medium ears before freezing whole; good for cornbread. |
| Figs | yes | yes | yes | |
| Grapes | | yes | yes | Good for baking. |
| Pears | yes | yes | yes | Can for sauces. |
| Peppers | yes | blanch first | yes | Blanch 3 minutes for halves before freezing; good for sauces and baked goods. |
| Tomatoes | yes | yes | yes | |

Most vegetables will need blanching before freezing. Blanching, which means to scald in boiling water for a very short time, brightens the color, helps retain more vitamins, and slows the action of enzymes that reduce flavor. Different vegetables require different blanching times. If you don't blanch long enough, you actually stimulate enzymes that speed deterioration.

To blanch, put clean, prepared vegetables in a wire basket (or a blanching basket) and drop this into a large pan of vigorously boiling water (you'll need about a gallon of water for every pound of prepared vegetables). Put a tight-fitting lid on the pan and as soon as the water returns to a vigorous boil, begin to time. Correct blanching time is critical. As soon as the right amount of time has elapsed, remove the basket of vegetables and drop it immediately into cold water. You want to cool the vegetables as quickly as possible (cooling should take about the same amount of time as blanching). Change the water or add ice as needed to keep it cold.

Certain vegetables, such as pumpkins, winter squash, and sweet potatoes, are best steam-blanched. This takes one and a half times as long as water-blanching, and you need a wire basket or steamer that sits about three inches above the boiling water. Otherwise, it's done the same way as water blanching.

Do not blanch in the microwave.

Once the vegetables have cooled, drain them thoroughly, then pack them in freezer containers and label with the date and contents.

## Special Handling

TOMATOES Drop cleaned tomatoes into boiling water for about 30 seconds, plunge into cold water, then slip off the skins. Pack cooled tomatoes into containers, leaving room for expansion, then label and freeze.

## Canning

Two things you should remember about canning fruits and vegetables: *do not* be intimidated by the idea of canning, and *do* follow the directions! Canning is a wonderful and safe way to preserve food, but you have to do it right. Some low-acid items, such as meats, need a steam pressure canner, but most produce can be processed with a water-bath canner.

**SWEET POTATOES, WINTER SQUASH, AND PUMPKINS** Cook until tender. Cool, peel, cut into chunks, and pack in a freezer container. Label and freeze.

**ZUCCHINI AND CARROTS** For baking, grate vegetables, steam for 1 to 2 minutes, then air-cool slightly. Measure the still-warm vegetables into quantities you would use for baking and place them in containers. Place the containers in cold water to continue to cool them, then label and freeze. When you are ready to use them, drain or wrap in a paper towel and remove as much moisture as possible.

### Rules

- Use jars made specifically for canning. Make sure they are not chipped or cracked.

- For canning, use *new* flat metal lids with rubber seals.

- Use *new* rings that twist around the top of the jars.

- Wash the jars and lids in hot, soapy water. Then place them in plain hot (but not boiling) water until you are ready to use them.

You can use a water canner or just a large pot with a tight-fitting lid. You will need a wire rack for the jars to sit on while being processed. It's also useful to have wide-mouth tongs for putting the jars into and taking them out of the boiling water.

## Canning Process

**1.** Fill the canner half full with water and place it over high heat. In a different pan, heat more water (1 or 2 quarts, depending on the size of the pan) and add the clean jars to sterilize them. Boil briefly. In a small saucepan, heat (but do not boil) the lids.

**2.** Prepare the food to be canned.

**3.** Remove the jars from the hot water and pour out any excess water.

**4.** Place these on a folded dish towel on the counter. Fill the jars with the prepared food, leaving a ¼-inch headspace for jams, jellies, and fruit sauces, and a ½-inch space for tomatoes, salsas, and pickles.

**5.** Clean the rims and threads of the jars with a clean, damp cloth.

**6.** Place a hot lid on each jar top, then twist on a metal ring.

**7.** Place the jars onto the wire rack in the canner. Be sure the jars are not touching each other or the bottom or sides of the pot.

**8.** Add the boiling water to the canner until the tops of the jars are covered with 1 to 2 inches of water.

**9.** When the water returns to a full rolling boil, begin timing. Processing time differs according to what is being canned. Be sure the jars are covered with water at all times.

**10.** When the processing is finished, remove the jars and place them on a folded dish towel on the counter to cool.

**11.** When the jars are cool, check to make sure they are sealed. If the lid does not move when pressed in, this indicates a proper seal. You must have a proper seal on your canned goods or else they will spoil.

## Processing Times

When two times are listed, the shorter times are for pints, the longer times for quarts. **Note:** *These times are for elevations of 1,000 feet or less. For every 1,000-foot elevation gain, add one minute.*

| Apples | 20 minutes |
|---|---|
| Berries (in syrup) | 15 minutes |
| Cranberry sauce | 5 minutes |
| Peaches (in syrup) | 15–20 minutes |
| Tomatoes | 35–40 minutes |
| Tomato sauce and salsa | 35–40 minutes |
| Jams and jellies | 5 minutes |

## Drying

You can use a conventional oven for drying fruits and vegetables, but it is much easier if you use a dehydrator.

However you choose to dry your produce, you need to start with firm, ripe, flavorful fruits and vegetables. Depending on what you're drying, some can be left whole with the peel on, and others should be peeled and cut into strips or pieces. Thin peeled pieces dry fastest. If you choose to leave the peel on, crack or break it in places so that it doesn't form an impenetrable layer that would slow the drying process. Be sure the fruit is clean and dry.

The idea is to dry the produce evenly so that the inside dries out at the same rate as the outside. This takes anywhere from several hours in a dehydrator to several weeks for air-drying. **Note:** *If you live in a humid region, it's going to be very difficult to air-dry food due to the amount of humidity in the air.*

Most people treat fruit intended for drying with sulfite or ascorbic acid (which is vitamin C) to help prevent it from turning dark; it also helps preserve it for a longer period of time.

Usually, fruits and vegetables do not dry evenly. The total moisture content should be about 20 percent, but this is distributed unevenly throughout the pieces. To redistribute the moisture and reduce the risk of developing mold, "condition" the items by cooling them, then packing them loosely in a glass jar. Allow this to sit for 8 to 10 days. Be sure to shake the jar every day to separate the pieces and check for condensation. The idea is that the drier parts will absorb moisture from the moister ones. If condensation begins to form, take out the fruit and dry it again in the oven, dehydrator, or sunlight.

Once the fruit is completely dry and cool, package it in moisture- and vapor-proof containers or glass jars. If you used sulfur as a pretreatment, be sure that this fruit does not touch metal, which can cause a color change in the fruit.

Properly dried fruit can be stored in a cool, dry place and will last for months, if not years. Every time you open the storage container, though, you let in moisture, so it's best to store fruit in amounts that you can use all at once.

One exception to the "difficult to dry in an oven" rule is the "sun"-dried tomato. The following recipe is tried-and-true, and is an excellent and beautiful way to use summer plum tomatoes. Try this in Rozanne Gold's Yellow Squash and Sun-dried Tomato "Quiche" (page 105).

# DRIED PLUM TOMATOES

1 cup light olive oil, plus more for coating the pan

6 plum tomatoes

1 teaspoon sea salt

3 to 4 sprigs fresh basil

Garlic clove (optional)

**1.** Preheat the oven to 200°F. Coat the bottom of a baking sheet with olive oil or cover it with a piece of foil.

**2.** Cut the tomatoes in half lengthwise.

**3.** Place a wire rack on top of the baking sheet.

**4.** Place the tomato pieces, skin side down, on the rack. Be sure that the tomato pieces do not touch and that there is plenty of space for air to circulate between them.

**5.** Sprinkle with the sea salt.

**6.** Place the baking sheet in the oven and leave the door slightly ajar.

**7.** Bake for about 6 hours, or until the tomatoes appear wrinkled, dry, and deep red. Do not allow them to crisp.

**8.** Remove the baking sheet from the oven and allow the tomatoes to cool thoroughly.

**9.** Pack them in a sterilized pint jar with the basil and garlic clove (if using). Pour the olive oil into the jar until the tomatoes and basil are completely covered.

**10.** Seal and store the jar in the refrigerator.

**Note:** *This is not processed and must be stored in the refrigerator. It will stay good for up to a week.*

# Growing Your Own

IF YOU WANT TO EAT ABSOLUTELY LOCALLY, YOU'LL NEED TO GROW AS many fruits and vegetables as you possibly can. Although many home gardeners have limited space and many urban gardeners must grow everything in containers, anyone can grow something to bake with. It's fun, the produce is absolutely delicious, and it's an inexpensive way to eat organically and locally.

One advantage to growing your own fruits and vegetables is that you have a huge number of varieties from which to choose. For example, your grocery store probably stocks only a few kinds of tomatoes (maybe nothing more than "big," "plum," "cherry," or "grape"), and these varieties were probably chosen for their ability to ship well and sit on a shelf without decaying for several days, rather than for their taste. Not surprisingly, vegetable varieties suitable for growing in a home garden have a far superior taste.

Although it's not in the scope of this book to give you detailed descriptions for planting and maintaining a home garden, the following ideas will give you a place to start. I've chosen these plants because they are (1) useful and (2) easy to grow in most regions. They might also be readily available at your local market, but, if you're interested in growing your own, this is a great place to start and will help reduce your carbon footprint.

· · · · · · ·

## Gardening Tips

The elements for a successful garden are pretty straightforward. You need good, rich soil, sunshine, and water. That's it! Of course you also need to choose herbs, fruits, and vegetables that grow well in your region, and you need to plant them during the correct season.

## Soil

This is the most important part of gardening. All the nutrients your plants receive come from the soil. However, native soils are rarely nutrient-rich enough to grow vegetables well. For small garden plots or containers, consider buying a rich topsoil or a soil mixture designed for container gardening. If you have a small space in your yard, think about building a raised bed. Rather than doing the tilling and mixing necessary to cultivate the land, simply fill the bed with good soil and plant immediately.

### Sun

Most "crops"—whether fruit, vegetable, or herb—perform best in full sun. If you don't have a sunny spot, you're going to be limited in what you can grow. If you're dedicated enough, you can grow things in containers and move them to catch the most sun, but the fact remains: You need a lot of sunlight to get a lot of produce.

### Water

Ideally, water comes in gentle, regular rains so you can just sit back and watch things grow. In actuality, this rarely happens (at least in most regions), meaning you'll need to supplement the amount of moisture your plants receive by watering regularly.

### Other Hints

A couple of other hints: Start small and don't try to plant a large garden unless you have lots of time and patience— and money. Especially if you're a new gardener, start with small seedlings rather than trying to grow things from seeds (exceptions noted below). And finally . . . just have fun with it. You're not a farmer (yet), so this is all to enhance your love of good, seasonal food. If your harvest isn't abundant the first year, don't worry about it—just supplement from your local market, but make notes about what worked and what didn't and make guesses as to why, so next year *you* can have a booth at the farmers' market!

## GMB Garden Favorites

The following fruits, vegetables, and herbs grow in most regions, are easy to grow in backyard gardens, and are great for using in a variety of baked goods.

BASIL If I could grow just one plant to use in baking, it would be basil. It's easy to grow and continues to produce abundantly throughout the growing season. Even better, it's easy to start from seeds and grows well in pots or in the ground almost anywhere in the United States and beyond. You can use it in many different recipes, from Pesto Pizza with Goat Cheese and Figs (see page 100) to Tomato, Goat Cheese, and Basil Cornbread (see page 104); it's sure to be a staple in your kitchen.

Plant basil in full sun. It is very sensitive to frost, so be sure that you wait until the weather has warmed before setting it out. If you start with seeds, plant them in shallow furrows and cover with half an inch of soil, or start the seeds indoors three to four weeks before the last predicted frost. Plant seedlings (or thin your garden seedlings) about 12 to 18 inches apart when they have developed two sets of leaves. Be sure to keep them moist. If they dry out, they will not grow as vigorously.

BLUEBERRIES Blueberries grow on a bush, either a low one or a high one (these are not just descriptions; they are also names and designations). Like other fruits and vegetables, blueberries need several hours of sunlight every day for the best yield. However, they will grow and produce fruit in light shade. Blueberry bushes prefer slightly acidic soils. If you are unsure about the pH of your soil, have a soil test done. (A soil test is recommended for backyard gardening.)

Be sure to plant more than one variety of blueberry bushes for cross-pollination and better yield. A total of four or five bushes should be enough to supply ample fruit for a family of four to eat all they want during the harvest season. To extend the season, plant different varieties that ripen at different times.

**FIGS** Figs need 6 to 8 hours of sunlight every day. Although they are considered more drought-tolerant than other fruits, they still benefit from at least an inch of rainfall every week. Plant figs in the spring before leaves start to emerge. Don't fertilize or prune at this time, just allow the plant to grow for the first season. After the first year or two, the shrubs benefit from an annual pruning where up to one-third of the plant is removed. Mature fig trees are about 10 feet tall with a span of 10 feet. Figs can tolerate temperatures down to about 10°F

to 20°F, but are not suitable for growing in cold climates. If the figs exude a milky sap, they are not quite mature, but they can still be picked and allowed to ripen off the plant.

**SWISS CHARD** Even though lettuce is probably the easiest leafy green to grow, I try to grow things such as arugula and Swiss chard as well, because they are used in baking recipes such as frittatas and quiches.

There are many advantages to growing Swiss chard. It tolerates both summer heat and cool weather, and it's pretty enough to grow as an ornamental, especially varieties with brightly colored stems. When harvesting, cut the leafy parts off the thick, tough stem. Soak the seeds overnight before sowing them directly into garden beds.

**ROSEMARY** Fortunately, you can find rosemary varieties that withstand both hot and cold conditions, making it possible to grow this incredibly useful herb in most regions of the country. Most varieties grow about four feet tall, with a similar width, and they need full sun and moist, well-drained soil. It does not tolerate drought or soggy conditions. Water regularly but moderately. Other than that, it's pretty easy to grow. It is a perennial, meaning that once you get it established, you should have it for years. In most regions, you can harvest rosemary leaves throughout the year from well-established plants.

STRAWBERRIES There are three main categories of strawberries: June-bearing, which produces one large crop of big berries every (surprise!) June; ever-bearing, which yields two or three smaller harvests during spring, summer, and fall; and day neutral, which produces fruit throughout the growing season. The latter two are great for small gardens because they do not put out many runners (small stems from the parent plant that root, thus multiplying your original plant many times over). Though runners might sound like a good thing, if you have a small space, it can get out of hand.

Strawberries need full sun and well-drained, rich garden soil. Be sure to water regularly and apply a thick layer of mulch around the plants to keep the berries from coming in contact with the soil.

TOMATOES Whether you choose heirloom, plum, Beefeater, yellow, orange, or bite-size tomatoes, if you can pick it off the vine and eat it right away, you'll be thrilled and delighted with the taste.

With the current popularity of heirloom tomatoes and the hefty price tag that's attached at the farmers' market, you might want to consider putting in at least one heirloom tomato plant. Heirloom vegetables are older varieties not used in large commercial operations. They are open-pollinated, meaning that they are not hybrids and that you can collect seeds to plant again. Try planting heirlooms such as Brandywine, Cherokee Purple, Green Zebra, Mortgage Lifter, and Red Pear.

No matter which varieties you choose to grow, all tomatoes basically require the same growing conditions, and first among these is full sun. Set out the plants after the danger of frost has passed and plant deeply, so that the lowest leaves are only about two inches from the ground. Be sure that the soil is rich and contains lots of compost and other amendments. Tomatoes benefit from occasional feeding, so find an organic fertilizer that is good for vegetables and apply according to the directions. Provide support by means of a tomato cage or stakes. Be sure to irrigate regularly so the soil stays evenly moist.

ZUCCHINI A perfect plant for people who lack a green thumb, zucchini is one of those plants that seems to take on a life of its own to produce prodigious amounts. Fortunately, you can use zucchini in a variety of baked goods (try our Zucchini Spice Muffins on page 97) and even freeze what you can't use right away. Plant in full sun, be sure to put it in a space where it can sprawl and grow, and watch out for pests and diseases from the get-go. Vine borers, in particular, can be devastating to the plant.

# Appendix

## Resources

We don't want anything to slow you down when you're ready to start baking naturally. The following resources might help you find what you need.

### Finding a Farmers' Market

According to the USDA, there are now more than 5,200 farmers' markets in the United States—and I bet they've missed a few! There has been an explosion of interest in farmers' markets, meaning they're popping up like weeds all over, full of delicious, locally grown, and (hopefully) organic produce. Try the following websites to find farmers' markets by state or zip code:

- Agricultural Marketing Service: www.ams.usda.gov
- BigBarn (United Kingdom): www.bigbarn.co.uk
- Farmers' Markets Canada: www.farmersmarketcanada.ca
- Local Harvest: www.localharvest.org

If you still can't find what you're looking for, call your county cooperative extension office for help.

In addition to markets, CSAs—or Community Supported Agriculture groups—are also gaining in number and popularity. These are organizations in which a farmer or a group of farmers are supported psychologically and financially by their communities. People in the region pledge to pay farmers a certain amount of money every week in return for seasonal produce. It's a great, beneficial situation for everyone involved. Try the following websites to find a CSA in your area:

- Biodynamic Farming and Gardening Association: www.biodynamics.com/csa
- Eat Well Guide: www.eatwellguide.org
- Local Harvest: www.localharvest.org

To find a farm where you can pick your own fruits or vegetables, try www.pickyourown.org. It includes state listings for all fifty states and offers information about harvest dates, farms (by region), markets, and festivals. In addition, it has some great tips for canning and preserving.

### Organic Baking Supplies

We highly recommend buying locally whenever you can, but we know that sometimes that's not possible. The following Web sites are listed for your consideration and convenience. *These websites are not recommendations or endorsements.*

#### General
- Eden Organic: www.edenfoods.com
- Manna Harvest Health Foods: www.mannaharvest.net

## Sweeteners
- Madhava Honey:
  www.madhavahoney.com
- Maple Syrup Store:
  www.maplesyrupstore.com
- Volcanic Nectar:
  www.volcanicnectar.com

## Nuts, Seeds, and Dried Fruits
- Diamond Organics:
  www.diamondorganics.com
- Nuts Online:
  www.nutsonline.com
- Tierra Farm:
  www.tierrafarm.com
- Wilderness Family Naturals:
  www.wildernessfamilynaturals.com

## Flours and Grains
- Anson Mills:
  www.ansonmills.com
- Bob's Red Mill:
  www.bobsredmill.com

## Chocolate
- Dagoba Organic Chocolate:
  www.dagobachocolate.com
- SunSpire:
  www.sunspire.com

## Helpful Organizations
- Edible Communities Publications:
  www.ediblecommunities.com
- Edible Schoolyard:
  www.edibleschoolyard.org
- Environmental Working Group:
  www.ewg.org
- Farm to Table:
  www.farmtotablenm.org
- Slow Food USA:
  www.slowfoodusa.org
- Weston A. Price Foundation:
  www.westonaprice.org

# Sample Menus

## Spring Lunch
Asparagus Flan with Smoked Salmon
    Potato Salad (page 62)
Spring greens
Sweet Strawberry Pie (page 54)

## Spring Brunch
Asparagus-Ricotta Tart with
    Comté Cheese (page 60)
Spelt Scones (page 178)
Apricot Squares (page 50)

## Summer Brunch
Farm eggs
Fresh fruit (peaches, berries, figs, etc.)
Lemon Ricotta Pancakes with Blueberries
    (page 174)
Maple syrup

## Summer Dinner
Green beans
Honey Whole Wheat Bread (page 56)
Yellow Squash and Sun-dried Tomato "Quiche"
    (page 105)
Blackberry Tart (page 89)

## Summer Dessert Party
English Fruit Trifle (page 79)
Huckleberry Sour Cream Pie (page 91)
Mexican Chocolate Cake with Vegan Mexican
    Ganache or Cinnamon Cream Cheese
    Maple Icing (page 162)
Peach and Nectarine Upside-down Cake
    (page 82)
Simpson County Watermelon Sorbet (page 109)

## Fall Pie Party
Lemon Raspberry Tart (page 172)
Nick's Favorite Apple Pie (page 124)
Pecan Pie (page 129)
Pumpkin Pie and Custard (page 130)

## Fall Cookout
Rustic Grilled Pizza (page 146)
Grilled harvest vegetables
Salad
All-Organic Special Occasion Cake
    with honey poached pears (page 76)

## Winter Brunch
Citrus fruits and fresh coconut
Fig and Blueberry Scones (page 96)
Vegetable Frittata with Potato Crust (page 61)
Orange-scented Chocolate Cupcakes with
    Chocolate Frosting (page 161)

## Winter Holiday Dessert Party
Cookies: Chocolate Chip, Thumbprint, Honey
    Fig Bars, (pages 31, 87 and 166)
Lemon Raspberry Tart (page 172)
Mexican Chocolate Cake with Vegan Mexican
    Ganache or Cinnamon Cream Cheese
    Maple Icing (page 162)
New York–style Cheesecake (page 78)

## Great Gifts
Applesauce (page 148)
Applesauce Walnut Bread (page 134)
Blueberry Ginger Sauce (with note to refrigerate)
    (page 107)
Chocolate Cupcakes (page 118)
Cranberry Coconut Granola (page 183)
Granola Bars (page 122)
Honey Fig Bars (page 166)
Honey Strawberry Jam (page 68)
Soft Pretzels (page 180)

## Kids' Party
Chocolate-covered Graham Crackers
    (page 51)
Chocolate Tofu Pudding (page 170)
Soft Pretzels (page 180)
Teething Biscuits (page 52)

# Recipes by Theme

# Contributor Biographies

### TERESE ALLEN

Terese Allen is food editor for the Organic Valley Family of Farms Web site, a cooperative of farmers working together since 1988 to keep its member families farming. Terese is the author of many cookbooks and a teacher and lecturer on "conscious eating." She has a passion for the places where "real food" happens, like farmers' markets, food festivals, cheese factories, diners, butcher shops, and, above all, home kitchens. www.tereseallen.com, www.organicvalley.coop

### SUSAN BALDASSANO

Susan Baldassano is an instructor and the director of education at the Natural Gourmet Institute for Health and Culinary Arts. She is also the founder and director of "To Grandmother's House We Go Cooking Tours." For the past twelve years she has coordinated a popular cooking demo class at the Park Slope Food Coop in Brooklyn, New York. www.tograndmothershousewego.com

### DAN BARBER

Dan Barber is executive chef and co-owner of Blue Hill (which received a *New York Times* three-star review) and Blue Hill at Stone Barns in Pocantico Hills, New York. In the summer of 2002, *Food and Wine* magazine featured Dan as one of the country's best new chefs. In May 2004, both Blue Hill at Stone Barns and Stone Barns Center for Food and Agriculture opened their doors. Dan helped create the philosophical and practical framework for the Center and guides it in its mission to create a consciousness about the effects of everyday food choices. Dan addresses local food system issues through op-eds in the *New York Times* and stories in *Gourmet* and *Food and Wine*. His writing has been incorporated into *Best Food Writing* in 2004, 2005, 2006, and 2007. www.bluehillfarm.com

### SUSAN BELSINGER

Susan Belsinger is a culinary herbalist and educator, food writer, and photographer who has authored or co-authored eighteen books and has been published in more than twenty-five national magazines and newspapers. She is passionate about her work—sharing the joy of gardening and cooking through teaching and writing—and inspiring others to get in touch with their senses of smell and taste. www.susanbelsinger.com

### AMY BESA AND ROMY DOROTAN

Amy Besa and Romy Dorotan started their critically acclaimed Filipino restaurant, Cendrillon, in 1995, then in 2009 revived it as The Purple Yam in Brooklyn. Amy and Romy are the authors of the cookbook *Memories of Philippine Kitchens* (2006). www.cendrillon.com

## BOB'S RED MILL

Bob Moore started his business in a historic flour mill near Oregon City, Oregon, to preserve the ancient craft of stone milling and to grind whole grains for the local community. Bob and his wife, Charlee, searched America for special stones used in century-old mills that would become the company's foundation for milling simple, wholesome, whole-grain foods. They overcame a devastating fire in 1988 and then, at nearly sixty years of age, Bob rebuilt his company in Milwaukie, Oregon, using the stones saved from the fire. www.bobsredmill.com

## MELISSA BREYER

Melissa Breyer is a food writer and editor who lives in Brooklyn, New York. Her work has appeared in national and international books and periodicals. She is the senior editor for the Web site Care2 Healthy and Green Living. The recipes Melissa contributed to the *Green Market Baking Book* originally appeared on www.care2.com.

## MARLENE BUMGARNER

Marlene is the author of several cookbooks about organic foods and whole grains. In 1976 she published *The Book of Whole Grains*. This was followed by *Organic Cooking for (Not-So-Organic) Mothers* in 1980. She wrote a weekly natural foods cooking column for the *San Jose Mercury* from 1976 until 1986, as well a monthly food and festivals column for *Mothering* magazine. *The New Book of Whole Grains* was published in 1997.

## CHRISTINE CARROLL

Christine is a scientist-turned-chef who now considers the kitchen her lab. When not devouring local plums, she runs a recreational cooking school in Manhattan's Lower East Side. She is also the founding director of CulinaryCorps, a nonprofit service organization for cooks. She lives on Roosevelt Island with her husband and her cookbooks. www.culinarycorps.org

## DELIA CHAMPION

When Delia Champion was young, her family lived above the restaurant they owned in southern New Jersey, and since that time, Delia has known she would do something with food. She moved to Atlanta in 1983 and, after years of working (very happily!) as a server at Indigo Coastal Grill and other fine Atlanta restaurants, she opened The Flying Biscuit Café in 1993. "I wanted to give people a place to get a really good breakfast before work," she said, "a place steeped in Southern flavor and Southern flair." The café was wildly successful and is now franchised. Together, all the locations make about five thousand biscuits every morning. www.flyingbiscuit.com

## CHEF ANN COOPER

Chef Ann Cooper is a renegade lunch lady. She works to turn cafeterias into culinary classrooms for students, one school lunch at a time. She has transformed public school cafeterias in New York City, Harlem, and Bridgehampton, New York, and now in Berkeley, California, teaching children why good food choices matter by putting

innovative strategies to work and providing fresh organic lunches to all students. Chef Ann's newest book is *Lunch Lessons: Changing the Way We Feed Our Children* (2006).
www.chefann.com
www.lunchlessons.org

## NICK COWLES

Shelburne Orchards has been in Nick Cowles's family since the 1950s. Located on the shores of Lake Champlain in Shelburne, Vermont, the orchard has more than eighty acres of apple trees, ten acres of which are designated organic. Nick has been overseeing growing and production for about thirty years.
www.shelburneorchards.com

## BEVERLY COX

Beverly Cox is the food editor of *Native Peoples* magazine and a former food editor and director of food styling for *Cook's Illustrated*. She holds a grand diplôme from Le Cordon Bleu in Paris and apprenticed with Gaston LeNotre. She has written twelve cookbooks, including *Spirit of the Harvest: North American Indian Cooking*. She has won James Beard and Julia Child/IACP awards for her books.

## ELIZABETH CRANE

Elizabeth Crane began working at the Ferry Plaza Farmers Market in San Francisco in 1994, when her first son was a year old. Fitzgerald's Premium Stone Fruit quickly became "the stand with the baby," and Elizabeth became "Stone Fruit Woman," a peach-loving superhero who freely dispensed recipes and advice on how to

select and prepare a dazzling array of peaches, nectarines, apricots, and pluots. A mother of two, Elizabeth now works as a freelance writer and as the manager of the Noe Valley Farmers' Market.

## CULINARYCORPS

Under the leadership of Christine Carroll, CulinaryCorps designs, organizes, and launches outreach experiences for culinary students and professional chefs. CulinaryCorps provides opportunities for those with a passion for and dedication to food to use their skills to help communities in need. Currently, their efforts are centered on the culinary renaissance of New Orleans, Louisiana, and the Gulf Coast of Mississippi. Their intention is to not only offer assistance to a community in need, but also to expose Corps members to the varied, vital, and often complex role that food plays in the well-being of a community.
www.culinarycorps.org

## DEBORAH LYNN DADD

Debra Lynn Dadd first wrote about natural sweeteners in 1984 in her groundbreaking self-published book on household toxics, *Nontoxic & Natural*. After living a nontoxic life for twenty years, she found that the one substance harmful to health that she had not removed from her life was refined white sugar. When Debra discovered she was diabetic, she began to study and experiment with natural sweeteners. Today she has more than two hundred recipes on her Web site and continues to explore new ideas about how we can enjoy sweets in a healthy way.
www.sweetsavvy.com

## TOM DOUGLAS

Tom Douglas, along with his wife and business partner, Jackie Cross, owns five of Seattle's most exciting restaurants, including Dahlia Lounge (nominated for Best Restaurant by the James Beard Association in 2006), Etta's, Palace Kitchen (nominated for Best New Restaurant by the James Beard Association in 1997), Lola, and Serious Pie. Tom is author of several cookbooks, including *Tom Douglas' Seattle Kitchen* (2000). www.tomdouglas.com

## CRESCENT DRAGONWAGON

Crescent Dragonwagon, the James Beard Award-winning author of *Passionate Vegetarian* (2002), grew up in the South but now lives in Vermont. There she writes (fiction, children's books, and, of course, cookbooks), cooks, gardens, plays with her cats, performs improv comedy, and blogs at "Nothing is wasted on the writer" (crescentdragonwagon.typepad.com). She prepared brunch for 1,200 people at Bill Clinton's first presidential inauguration, and has served cornbread not only to the president, but to titled royalty, a World Series of Poker champion, and a world-renowned feminist. www.dragonwagon.com

## EDEN FOODS

Eden Foods has been an independent manufacturer of organic, traditional, and natural foods for forty years. Seventy-seven percent of Eden Foods are North American family-farm grown. Eighty-two percent are certified organic, and ninety-six percent are kosher and pareve. Eden uses no irradiation, no preservatives, no toxic additives, no food colorings, no refined sugars, and no genetically engineered ingredients. www.edenfoods.com

## FARMER JOHN AND ANGELIC ORGANICS

"Farmer John," aka John Peterson, is a successful Chicago-area organic grower and the head of Angelic Organics, a Community Supported Agriculture (CSA) program in the Chicago area. He is the subject and co-producer of the documentary *The Real Dirt on Farmer John* and the author of *Farmer John's Cookbook: The Real Dirt on Vegetables* (2006). www.angelicorganics.com

## MARTHA HALL FOOSE

Martha Hall Foose is executive chef of the Viking Cooking School. Born and raised in the Mississippi Delta, she attended the famed pastry school École Lenôtre in France. When she returned to Mississippi, she opened Bottletree Bakery in Oxford and later, with her husband, Mockingbird Bakery in Greenwood. She lives with her husband and their son in Tchula, Mississippi and is the author of *Screen Doors and Sweet Tea* (2008). www.marthafoose.com

## ROZANNE GOLD

Four-time James Beard Award winner Rozanne Gold is one of the most prominent women in the food world. At the age of twenty-three, she was the first chef to New York City's Mayor Ed Koch and she became a pioneer for women entering the field. She is chef-director of the renowned consulting group The Joseph Baum & Michael

Whiteman Co., best known for creating the Rainbow Room, Windows on the World, and five of New York's three-star restaurants. An accomplished food writer, Ms. Gold is the author of twelve cookbooks and was the home entertaining columnist for *Bon Appetit* magazine. She has inspired home cooks and professional chefs alike to "keep it simple." www.rozannegold.com

### RONIT GOURARIE

Ronit Gourarie has been making bread her whole life and has been teaching bread making at PCC Natural Markets in Seattle since 2002. She holds a master's degree in nutrition from Bastyr University. She has a passion for nutrition and food, with a special focus on how everyday eating impacts health and well-being.

### ANN HARMAN

Ann Harman is an international bee consultant, having gone to twenty-six developing nations on five continents, offering hands-on assistance to beekeeping groups. She is the co-author of *The ABC & XYZ of Bee Culture* (2007) and writes for *Bee Culture*, *Beekeeper Quarterly*, and *Bee Craft* magazines.

### MARK HASKELL

Mark Haskell lives in Washington, DC, and Buisson, France. He is founder of Friends & Food International, a culinary travel and consulting company, and has cooked in restaurants in Asia, Europe, and North and South America. He was knighted in 2007 to the Confrérie de Saint-Vincent in France for his work with Slow Food and biodynamic and organic winemakers.

### HOPE'S GARDENS

Hope's Gardens was formed over the summer of 2007, and the owners have spent virtually every weekend since then at the local farmers' markets selling pesto and have developed a loyal following. www.hopesgardens.com

### LINTON HOPKINS

Linton Hopkins is Atlanta's premier farm-to-table chef. He is owner and executive chef of Restaurant Eugene and co-owner of Holman and Finch Public House and the H and F bakery, all of which espouse the idea of fresh, local, and seasonal cooking. He is actively involved with the Edible School Yard program and was instrumental in starting the Peachtree Farmers' Market in Atlanta. In 2009, he won a *Food & Wine Magazine* Best New Chef Award.

### ALEXANDRA JAMIESON

Alexandra Jamieson is a holistic health counselor and personal chef who works with individual clients all over the world. She graduated from both the Institute for Integrative Nutrition and New York City's Natural Gourmet Cookery School and has appeared on *Oprah*, *30 Days*, *The National Health Test* with Bryant Gumble, and the award-winning documentary *Super Size Me*. Her book *The Great American Detox Diet* (2005) offers sane, tasty advice on how to clean out, feel great, and live healthfully. www.healthychefalex.com

## LINDA JOHNSON AND MICHAEL JOHNSON

Formerly involved in the restaurant industry, Linda Johnson and Michael Johnson bought Sylvan Falls Mill Bed and Breakfast in Rabun County, Georgia, in 2001. The Mill itself is 167 years old, and the Johnsons use it to mill their own grain two or three times a week. www.sylvanfallsmill.com

## SONYA JONES

For Sonya Jones, baking is a family experience. She learned to bake from her mother, who ran a soul food restaurant in Atlanta, where Sonya grew up as one of ten children. Today she owns and runs the Sweet Auburn Bread Company in Atlanta, where she is assisted by her son Bobby. www.sweetauburnbread.com

## MEREDITH McCARTY

Meredith McCarty has been a vegan and macrobiotic cookbook author, teacher, speaker, and counselor since 1977. Formerly the associate editor of *Natural Health* magazine, Meredith co-directed a macrobiotic natural health center in northern California for nineteen years. Her book *Sweet & Natural* (1999) won an international cookbook award. www.healingcuisine.com

## MICHELLE McKENZIE

Michelle McKenzie graduated from the University of North Carolina at Chapel Hill with a degree in nutrition and a minor in chemistry. She then became immersed in health-supportive cuisine at the Natural Gourmet Institute for Health and Culinary Arts in New York City. It is this unique educational background, along with her extensive knowledge of healing cuisines and her passion for local and artisanal products, that shapes her perspective on food choices and preparation.

## SABRINA MODEL-CARLBERG

Sabrina Model-Carlberg was raised in a French family in the San Francisco Bay Area. Her food reflects her upbringing as well as her belief that the farmers' market is the happiest place on earth. She still lives in the Bay Area with her husband and their menagerie of pets.

## CARRIE NAHABEDIAN

Over the past twenty-four years, Carrie Nahabedian has developed a cooking style that combines her Armenian roots with influences from California, where she was executive chef for the Four Seasons Resort Santa Barbara and Beverly Hills properties. She returned to her native Chicago and joined forces with her cousin, Michael, to open the highly acclaimed Naha restaurant. Proof of her success and her growing influence in the restaurant world came when she won the James Beard Foundation Best Chef Great Lakes in 2008. www.naha-chicago.com

## NATIONAL HONEY BOARD

The National Honey Board (NHB) conducts research and helps to expand domestic and foreign markets for honey. The Board supports the education and enrichment of individual beekeepers throughout the country, offers information to consumers, researches new ways to use honey in foods and other products, helps beekeepers with merchandising, and promotes honey overseas. www.honey.com

## NATIONAL SWEET SORGHUM PRODUCERS AND PROCESSORS ASSOCIATION

Sorghum, sometimes seen as sorghum molasses, is 100 percent pure and natural juice extracted from sorghum cane. The syrup retains all of its natural sugars and other nutrients and is a great local sweetener for those fortunate enough to live in the southeastern United States, where it is most often produced. The NSSPPA is dedicated to educating people about the many uses of sorghum. www.ca.uky.edu/nssppa

## COLLEEN PATRICK-GOUDREAU

Determined to raise awareness about animal suffering, Colleen Patrick-Goudreau founded the organization Compassionate Cooks, which serves as a voice for the more than 45 billion land and sea animals killed every year in the United States for human consumption. Colleen has appeared on the Food Network, is a columnist for *VegNews Magazine*, and is also a contributor on National Public Radio. She is the author of *The Joy of Vegan Baking* (2007).

## CHRISTINA PIRELLO

Christina Pirello is the Emmy Award-winning host of the nationally aired PBS television series *Christina Cooks*. She has taught whole foods cooking classes and conducted lifestyle seminars on the power

of food for over fifteen years. Cooking with her mother as a child, Christina's relationship with food led to work as a pastry chef and caterer. Following her diagnosis of leukemia at the age of twenty-six, Christina's attention became focused on the connection between food and wellness as she turned to whole foods to help cure her disease. www.christinacooks.com

## JESSICA PRENTICE

Jessica Prentice is a professional chef, local foods activist, and author. Her first book, *Full Moon Feast: Food and the Hunger for Connection* (2006), follows the thirteen moons of a traditional agrarian calendar through the year. Jessica coined the word *locavore* and, in 2006, she joined four partners in founding Three Stone Hearth, a community-supported kitchen that uses local, sustainable ingredients to prepare nutrient-dense traditional foods on a community scale. She lives, works, and writes in the San Francisco Bay Area. www.threestonehearth.com

## EVAN PRICE

Evan Price started the Blue Heron Bakery in 1977 with the goal to supply the Olympia, Washington, community with whole-grain, organic baked goods. The bakery continues its commitment to helping create a healthier world. Blue Heron Bakery is a member of the Provender Alliance, a natural-foods educational organization comprised of manufacturers, distributors, and retailers of natural foods in the northwestern United States. www.blueheronbakery.com

## JODI RHODEN

Jodi Rhoden is originally from Marietta, Georgia. She continues to draw on the memories and recipes of the great Southern cooks and bakers in her family to create new recipes for Short Street Cakes, her specialty wedding, birthday, and cupcake bakery in Asheville, North Carolina. Jodi grows organic, edible flowers and herbs to decorate and flavor her cakes and loves using locally produced flours, eggs, and fruits in her creations. www.shortstreetcakes.com

## DAVID ROMINES

David Romines has spent more than twenty-five years in the food industry and is passionate about teaching people about good food. He says that he now focuses his attention on telling people of all walks of life about Slow Food and why it is so important.

## CHARLES SANDERS

Charles Sanders has lived in the rugged wooded hills of southern Indiana all his life. Persimmons are a common wild fruit in those parts and are used in cookies, pudding, bread, and even wine. His interest in using persimmons comes from his grandmother's wonderful persimmon pudding. Charles is the author of *The Self-Reliant Homestead* (2003).

## SCHERMER PECANS

The Schermer Pecan Company was started in southern Georgia in 1946 by Alton and Lula Schermer to provide quality products to be sold as fund-raisers for church and civic groups. Frank Wetherbee bought the company in 1977 and began offering the products commercially as well. www.schermerpecans.com

## KATHERINE SCHLOSSER

Kathy Schlosser has been a member of the Herb Society of America since 1990, and was formerly the chair of the National Herb Garden at the U.S. National Arboretum in Washington, DC. She is the editor of the Herb Society's *The Essential Guide to Growing and Cooking with Herbs* (2007), and she writes for local and national magazines, newspapers, and journals.

## BEV SHAFFER

Chef Bev Shaffer's signature humor and accessible teaching style shows through in all her culinary endeavors as a columnist, instructor, and author. Bev has written *No Reservations Required* (2003), *BROWNIES to Die For!* (2006), and *Mustard Seed Market & Café Natural Foods Cookbook* (2007). www.bevshaffer.com

## NICKI SIZEMORE

Nicki Sizemore graduated from the French Culinary Institute in New York City and is currently food editor for *Organic Wine Journal*. She has written for other publications and has worked in the test kitchens of *Saveur* and *Everyday with Rachael Ray*. She teaches cooking to both adults and teenagers with a focus on healthful, seasonal cooking. www.nickisizemore.com

## SUSAN SPICER

Susan Spicer and Regina Keever opened the restaurant Bayona in the French Quarter of New Orleans in 1990 and soon won national awards and recognition. In May 1993, Susan won the James Beard Award for Best Chef Southeast and, in 1995, was chosen for the Mondavi Culinary Excellence Award. Her first cookbook is *Crescent City Cooking* (2007). www.bayona.com

## MOLLY STEVENS

Molly Stevens is a food writer, editor, cooking teacher, and author of *All About Braising: The Art of Uncomplicated Cooking* (2004). Molly serves on the board of directors of Vermont Fresh Network and lives near Burlington, Vermont. www.mollystevenscooks.com

## U.S. HIGHBUSH BLUEBERRY COUNCIL

The U.S. Highbush Blueberry Council consists of growers and packers in North and South America who market their blueberries in the United States. www.blueberry.org

## VOLCANIC NECTAR COMPANY

Volcanic Nectar, headquartered in Utah, specializes in agave nectar. Agave nectar is made from the agave plant, a succulent that grows in the desert. A mature agave has leaves five to eight feet tall, is seven to twelve feet in diameter, and will live for eight to fifteen years. Volcanic Nectar's products are made from agave plants grown in Mexico. www.volcanicnectar.com

## CAROL ANNE WASSERMAN

Carol Anne Wasserman is a certified holistic health counselor with a private practice in Manhattan. She specializes in helping people with permanent weight loss and healing through macrobiotics and natural foods. www.gethealthywithcarol.com

## ALICE WATERS

Alice Waters started Chez Panisse restaurant in Berkeley, California, in 1971. Her philosophy was to serve the highest quality products only when they were in season. Chez Panisse was voted the best restaurant in America in 2001 and Alice was voted one of the ten best chefs in the world in 1986. She is an advocate for farmers' markets and sustainable agriculture, and serves as an international governor of Slow Food. The Chez Panisse Foundation supports many projects, including Edible Schoolyard. www.chezpanissefoundation.org

## MELANIE WAXMAN

As a mother of seven children, all raised on a grain-based diet without animal and dairy food, Melanie Waxman has experienced firsthand what it means to make healthful food for a full house. A highly respected macrobiotic practitioner, she has been actively involved in the healing arts since the early eighties and specializes in balancing health through food and diet, in the body and in the home. She has written numerous books and articles about healthful food and eating, and currently maintains an active practice in Chester County, Pennsylvania. www.celebrate4health.com

## CYNTHIA WONG

Cynthia Wong began her career as the baker at Reed Heron's restaurant Lulu in San Francisco in the early nineties. From there, she continued her education with formal culinary training at École Lenôtre in Plaisir, France, earning the grande diplôme de la cuisine Française. Suffering from a severe case of wanderlust, she moved to Barcelona, Spain, where she was pastry chef at Reno Paradis before she switched gears to food writing for *Barcelona Metropolitan* magazine and *Time Out* travel guides. Cynthia was also the chef de cuisine and production manager of Via Elisa Fresh Pasta, sous chef and food stylist for TBS's *Dinner and a Movie*, *Creative Loafing*'s Cheap Eats columnist, and culinary production assistant/assistant food stylist for *Good Eats* before returning to her true love of baking and pastry at Cakes & Ale in Decatur, Georgia. Her desserts have been featured in *Food & Wine* magazine and called "matchless" by food writer Christiane Lauterbach.

## REBECCA WOOD

Rebecca Wood has taught and written about healing with a sustainable diet since 1970 and has established two cooking schools. Her book *The Splendid Grain* (1998) won both a James Beard Award and a Julia Child/IACP Award. Her most recent book, *The New Whole Foods Encyclopedia* (1999), was a One Spirit Book Club main selection. Rebecca's articles appear in various publications including *Ladies' Home Journal*, *Yoga Journal*, *Veggie Life*, *Men's Fitness*, *American Health*, and *Utne Reader*. www.rwood.com

## SELECTED BIBLIOGRAPHY

Bumgarner, Marlene. *The New Book of Whole Grains: More Than 200 Recipes Featuring Whole Grains.* New York: St. Martin's Griffin, 1997.

*Cook's Illustrated* magazine. *The New Best Recipe.* Brookline, Mass.: America's Test Kitchen, 2004.

Corriher, Shirley. *CookWise: The Secrets of Cooking Revealed.* New York: William Morrow, 1997.

Phaidon Press. *The Silver Spoon.* New York: Phaidon, 2005.

Fallon, Sally. *Nourishing Traditions: The Cookbook That Challenges Politically Correct Nutrition and Diet Dictocrats.* Washington, DC: New Trends Publishing, 2003.

Hensperger, Beth. *Bread.* San Francisco: Chronicle Books, 1988.

McCarty, Meredith. *Sweet and Natural.* New York: St. Martin's Press, 1999.

Nestle, Marion. *What to Eat.* New York: North Point Press, 2006.

Pitchford, Paul. *Healing with Whole Foods: Asian Traditions and Modern Nutrition.* Berkeley, Calif.: North Atlantic Books, 2002.

Wittenberg, Margaret M. *New Good Food: Essential Ingredients for Cooking and Eating Well.* Berkeley, Calif.: Ten Speed Press, 2007.

Wood, Rebecca. *The New Whole Foods Encyclopedia.* New York: Penguin Compass, 1999.

# Acknowledgments

This book would not have been possible without the generosity of our contributors. I am grateful to them for their enthusiastic support of this project. Thanks also to our friends and family, who were equally enthusiastic about serving as tasters and testers of all the recipes. I would like to offer special thanks to my agent, Jeanne Fredericks, and to my editor, Jennifer Williams, for her friendship and support throughout this project, and to Sasha Tropp for her impressive ability to juggle, soothe, nudge, and nurture this book into being. Thank you also to Melanie Gold for her thorough text copyedit; Elizabeth Mihaltse, who designed the beautiful cover; Christine Heun, who designed the fabulous interior; and Hannah Reich, project editor, who spent countless hours helping this book live up to its full potential.

# INDEX OF RECIPES AND INGREDIENTS